# MY LIFE AS A JEHOVAH'S

# WITNESS

# USED, ABUSED, and FORGOTTEN

My life As a Jehovah's Witness

Used, Abused, and Forgotten

The True Story of a Former JW

**Randolph G. Thomas**

ISBN 978-0-9843494-4-9

www.authorrandythomas.com

Dedication

In memory of my sister, Shirley Thomas Scott. This is her book in another sense as well; because her life made it possible, and because her death made it necessary.

A Tribute from Here to Heaven

I thought of you with love today
But that is nothing new
I thought about you yesterday
And days before that too
I think of you in silence
I often speak your name
Now all I have is memories
And your picture in a frame
Your memory is my keepsake
With which I'll never part
The Supreme Being has you in his keeping
I have you in my heart
If roses grow in heaven Lord
Please pick a bunch for me
Place them in my sister's arms
And tell here they're from me
Tell her I love her and miss her
And when she turns to smile
Place a kiss upon her cheek
And hold her for a while
Because remembering her is easy
I do it every day
But there is an ache within my heart
That will never go away

# Contents

# MY LIFE AS

# A

# JEHOVAH'S WITNESS

# USED, ABUSED, AND FORGOTTEN

# Introduction

My first vivid memory in life begins with the word *Jehovah*. As a child, everything I did was surrounded by that word; even when it came down to corporal punishment. At the time I was being raised, the *Watchtower*'s theme song was "Beat your children!" The organization has always encouraged corporal punishment, stating that spanking is for the good of the child, and holding back the rod of correction was not. I can clearly remember being whipped by my mother with an actual curtain rod in my early teens. It left many stripes, something I will never forget. She used this type of punishment out of a desire for control and to create fear in me.

If she was unsuccessful in using the curtain rod, she would try other cruel methods, like sitting on my head while whipping my young ass. I remember not being able to breathe and afraid that I would suffocate. If she wasn't beating the crap out of me, my father was constantly slicing me with his belt; belt buckle and all.

The emotional and physical abuse started at an early age and as I got older, I found that it had left deep, long-lasting, and hidden scars; anger and resentment. Down the road, this form of religious abuse would seriously interfere with my cognitive, emotional, social, and psychological development as well; especially when I turned older. My parents made it very clear to me that I couldn't accomplish anything in life unless I remained a Jehovah's Witness. So, no matter what I did in life to better myself, they were never around to acknowledge it, as long as it didn't represent the *Watchtower* society.

In life, many of us are born with certain talents; some, with the talent to think and reason. Being raised a Jehovah's Witness, my thinking capabilities became terminal. My parents had a backwards view on life, all provided by the teachings of the *Watchtower* Bible and Tract Society. They constantly drilled it in me to accept the teachings and to live a low state of existence while doing so. As you read my story, my object is to give a candid and truthful statement of facts; to repeat the story of my life without exaggeration. My story is basically a story of survival and determination. My mission is to write an account as accurately as possible with depth and emotion. In doing so, it made me relive the events repeatedly. My pen had to dodge the teardrops constantly.

Another way for me to take some power back is to share my story; bearing witness to the wrong. I believe it can help others who've experienced the same or worst by making it real.

This is a personal book. I do not represent myself as a spokesman for other family members. I will simply talk about my experiences of being raised as a Witness, first as a child, then a baptized teenager, to an excommunicated one, and then as a young man running wild, filled with intimate sexual escapades and empty romances. I lastly give my experience about returning to the organization, dating, and getting married to a Jehovah's Witness.

My story helps readers see the stages one may go through after joining the Jehovah's Witness organization. It demonstrates that Jehovah's Witnesses are not Christians in the true sense of the word, similar to that of what the word of God says, and that the theology with which they are concerned is not part of the framework of God's instructions concerning love for man.

I knew one day I would write this book. I would transform my experience and write it out of my own need to put into words some of the most important things I have come to believe, experience, and know. You who are reading my story must carefully count the cost when confronted with the temptation of joining this cult.

I've placed before you as much information about my experience as I can in a few pages in the hope that some of it may be clarifying, and maybe you can understand how I have arrived where I am today. Getting the word out may eventually spark the interest of many who probably never even realized such barbaric practices do exist. Having lived the cult life, I must make known how very real it is, how damaging it is from birth to adulthood. I believe that only through deeper awareness and understanding can we hope to cure the wounds that religious abuse causes.

I have also built this book around several ex-Jehovah Witnesses who lived and died in my lifetime. They were great people and in some ways, this book is their story. I have seen more pain from this cult on a personal level in my life, and also from others I have reconnected with after they left. I know of suicides either directly or indirectly because of the shunning and not being able to face the prospect of being shunned.

I hope it brings light and justice to those from whom lives were snatched in one single judgment by wolves in sheep's clothing. The story of my life is true; although I have changed the names of the people involved to hide their identity, for privacy purposes. Also, I'm sorry if some things in my story are too graphic. It is necessary in this narrative to present a full and truthful statement of all the principal events in the history of my life as a Jehovah's Witness; to portray the organization of the *Watchtower* Bible and Tract Society as I have seen and known it; cruel, unjust, barbarous. Here is my story.

# Chapter 1

# *Genesis*

My story begins in Jersey City, New Jersey. Naturally my parents figured in this, so let's start with them. My father, Samuel Thomas Jr., was born in Brooklyn, New York. He was the fourth child, with one younger sister. His parents were stowaways from the island of St. Kitts. I have very few memories of them, but do remember that they were kind to me.

My mother, Francis Blanch Thomas, was also born in Brooklyn, New York. Their exact birth dates are a mystery, something I shall explain as we move on. She was the fifth of seven children, and was born into a Baptist family with high values. Her father, William Monroe, worked for the post office and provided well for his family. He was a disciplinarian and ran a tight ship. Mom often referred to him as a mean person. He also took care of his blind mother. She died when I was nine years old.

My mother's mother, Blanch Monroe, was a housewife, and was much loved and well-respected by all. During my younger years, I remember her visiting us and baking delicious pies. We had a blackberry tree in our backyard and on occasion she would create magic with them. Other than that, I never got to fully know her because I was barred from visiting her because of religious differences. Both grandparents died when I was in my late twenties. I remember being ridden with guilt for not trying to visit her on my own free will over the years.

Getting back to my parents, there is a lot I don't know about their early upbringing. They were unaccustomed to speaking of their early life. One of the few things I can recall is that during their early years, they had a courtship my mother's father did not agree with. It is believed that he didn't trust my father, and knew he wasn't educated. He had put all his children through college, and most have had great careers.

My mother, on the other hand, did not finish her education, and during the courtship, became pregnant. They eloped and were married in a simple ceremony conducted by the justice of the peace. They then moved in with a close relative. Later, they found an apartment in the projects in Hoboken, New Jersey. This is where they found their feet, and where she gave birth to her first child.

After a while, they moved to a top-floor shotgun apartment in a two-story building in Jersey City, New Jersey. By that time, my mother had given birth to three other children. The block they moved on was named Randolph Avenue; this is where I was born, and was named Randolph Gregory Thomas.

As time moved on, our family grew larger. I believe this took a toll on my mother in the later years; her body wore down bearing children, many one year apart; one held in arm, a second tugging at her skirt, the third kicking in her womb.

There were now nine of us, the youngest being six months old. We were so poor that two of my sisters had to sleep in my mother's bedroom dresser drawer when they were born because we couldn't afford to buy a crib. We were all bunched up together in that small apartment. There were four small bedrooms and one small bathroom for the nine of us. We all had to share rooms together.

In our second-floor apartment, we had a wonderful view of New York Harbor and could see lower Manhattan. It didn't have the breathtaking skyline we see today. At nighttime, I was fascinated by the bright lights that bedecked the Staten Island ferry's railings; it was a spectacular sight to watch. We also had a great view of the Verrazano Bridge, Ellis Island, the Statue of Liberty, and Governor's Island. It was very pretty during sunset.

During the day, we watched the large sailboats cruise up and down the New York Harbor along with huge warships, and the Circle Line tourist vessel riding the small waves of the Hudson River. During that time, there was not much for us to do, and we didn't go anywhere except the backyard; that was our

2

playground. It was slanted, and during the winter when it snowed, we enjoyed riding down that slope and used a garbage can cover as a sled. All in all, it was fun. Our downstairs neighbors were our playmates. They also had a large family, eight in total, and we created a bond with their entire family.

During my early childhood, I remember Mom working part-time doing domestic work the nearby Holiday Inn. She also worked part-time for a food service at school. During the early 1960s, the government began a program called the free lunch program, something we were on. Mom worked on the assembly line, handing out box lunches to the students. The box lunches consisted of peanut butter and jelly sandwiches, cheese, and a carton of milk. She managed to bring some of that home for us. Our refrigerator was loaded with box lunches and that was our daily menu for a while until she resigned from work because of the demands at home.

She worked hard at home taking care of us, which was a full-time job. She had great physical strength and seemed never to tire. Back in the day, she did everything the old-fashioned way. She would wash clothes with a scrub board until Dad bought her a used Maytag washer.

She also did most of the shopping for the family. I remember her always taking me along with her. I was six years old at that time and loved being with her. At times, she was good to me. There was a place of business in Newark, New Jersey, called Pop's where she did most of her grocery shopping. This place sold damaged goods at half price. Whatever she bought, she made good use of it, and made sure we had at least three meals a day.

Dinnertime was Noodle Roni time. As far as I can remember, we were raised mostly on noodles, pork and beans, spaghetti, and beef franks. She had an assortment of different noodle products in the pantry; everything from Mueller's thin spaghetti to elbow macaroni, rotini, tortellini, rigatoni, and medium and large shells. We ate fried noodles with franks, boiled noodles with franks, scrambled noodles with eggs, and every variety of noodles. Since we ate noodles daily, and our downstairs neighbors were aware of it, they would tease us and refer to us as the noodle family.

While blessing the food, I could have sworn I heard Dad mutter these words, "Give us this day our daily noodles." Then again, times were hard, and feeding nine kids on Dad's small salary was no easy task; but she found a way. She did all she could to sustain us and it was much appreciated.

Dad was rarely at home. Most times, he was out trying to make a living for our family. He was a big man who made a living working as a truck delivery driver. When he was home, he was a tyrant. He was forever ordering Mom about and always arguing with her. Most of the time when they argued, they argued behind closed doors in their bedroom, and it was loud.

Childhood was a calendar of humdrum days slashed by the lightning of Dad's fury and the sting of his belt. In my family dynamic, he was the violent narcissist who demeaned and emotionally and physically abused me. He required absolute perfection and compliance from me. Perhaps that is why I always felt guilty about something; guilty for being too noisy, even when I wasn't very loud. Guilty for having needs and feelings. Guilty for being happy about something. Guilty for not having done enough to help around the house, and guilty for just existing. Up until this day I find myself feeling guilty about something I did or didn't do, always walking with my head down.

Anyway, he hurt me the most with his disinterest in me as a normal human being with needs. He was a bitter, empty, distant person, and his treatment of me defined me as not important and not valuable or loveable. There was never any relationship, and no dialogue other than harassment, unless I wanted to listen to him preach his obscure spiritual Jehovah's Witness philosophies to me.

When it came down to my mother, whenever I committed an infraction, she would use the old line of "wait until your father comes home" to put fear in me. Still occasionally I can hear those words that produced fear and dread in my young heart so many years ago. At that time, she was passive-aggressive and emotionally unavailable, as she was too busy dancing to his tune, ignoring and refusing to see the abuse. When being beaten by him, she just put her head down in silence. For the most part, in any situation in which I took issue with him I'd be up against both rather than just him. I would say that they enabled each other's abuse 99 percent of the time. However, when he was not around, she took her frustration out on me and crossed the danger edge of cruelty with her style of punishment.

Her favorite form of punishment was sitting on my head while whipping my ass. This she loved because it prevented me from moving or running away from her abuse. She would instruct me to get on my knees and rest my forehead on the bed, she would then turn around and sit on my head and start whipping my ass. During those beatings, I never felt any pain. My main objective was to breathe. I tried very hard to lift my head up for air because it felt like I was suffocating. I always wondered why she had to sit on my head; perhaps this form of punishment was like what she grew up with, and was the only thing she was familiar with.

When all of this was taking place, it was never a problem to feel the hurt and anger toward her for her cruelty, because it taught me to care more about other people's feelings than my own. It also made me understand that she let me down just as much in that moment as when he was kicking my ass as well. She let him do this to her child, and that gave the message that I wasn't worth protecting.

With Dad, I knew for a fact that I was afraid of him. I don't ever recall giving him any lip when I was young. Whenever he returned home from work, I stayed out of his sight out of fear that Mom would give him a bad report about something I had done during the day, and then I was in for it. I sustained countless nose bleeds after being slapped in the face by him for the slightest infraction. His form of discipline was either his hand or his leather belt. I would guess that I received many whippings that I don't remember. I also received some I remember clearly.

For example, when I was a kid I was always hungry and in our family, there was not much to eat due to financial constraints.

During that time, I had a love for bread. My mission was to steal a few slices on a daily basis, especially late at night when my parents fell asleep. At times, this was a mission impossible because I had to cross their bedroom, which was located right next to the kitchen. Since we lived in an old apartment the floors were very squeaky, especially in front of their bedroom. To be successful in my endeavor I had to navigate myself around that. It was hard to do that in the dark, but I managed.

Once successful, I grabbed what I could and had a feast. I enjoyed eating my take under the kitchen table. The perfect hiding place…so I thought. Suddenly, Dad appeared on the scene shining a flashlight in my face. I was caught red-handed and as I tried to escape, he took off one of his slippers and threw it at me. After catching up with me, he whipped me like a man.

My mother was just as brutal as he was. When I defied her authority, she had no trouble grabbing anything she could to whack me with. She also disciplined me with the curtain rod and switch. For example, one morning, she made some homemade biscuits that were simply delicious. One thing she could do the best was make biscuits from scratch. If she would have been allowed to go into business making biscuits, I believe she would have been successful. The perfect name for her business would have been Fran-Jangles.

Anyway, I set out a plan to steal some once I got the chance. Later that morning she headed out shopping, and that was my perfect chance. We were all in the living room watching cartoons while being watched by my oldest sister when I made my move. I managed to sneak into the kitchen and in searching for the biscuits, I found they were nowhere in sight. I searched the refrigerator and they weren't there, so I pulled a chair up to the stove and looked in the kitchen cabinets—and there they were. She had cleverly placed them in a jar out of my reach. Nevertheless, as small as I was, with great effort, I managed to get a few and hid them in my underwear.

Heading back to the living room I was confronted by my older sister, who wanted to know what I was doing in the kitchen. While giving her no excuse, she shoved me and ordered me back in the living room. Upon doing so, to her surprise, the biscuits fell out of my underwear onto the floor. When Mom got home and was given the news, it was blackberry switch time for me. She had me go handpick my own switch from our blackberry tree. I brought one back that wasn't to her liking and got whipped even harder. That afternoon, I wore many stripes. I was six years old at that time.

Once Dad heard the news, he thought I was being greedy, and that's what he nicknamed me, "Greedy." To me it seems that he didn't know the difference between being greedy and being hungry. Even after getting so many beatings from both parents, I continued to be a food bandit. No matter what, I was going to steal whatever food I could to satisfy my appetite. My parents and I had two different sets of messages when it came down to stealing food. Their message was, "Thou shall not steal." My message was, "Thou shall not go hungry." This was my harsh reality and memories from a difficult childhood.

Due to their religious beliefs while studying to become Jehovah's Witnesses, they thought that God not only supported frequent corporal punishment, but encouraged it. The *Watchtower* Society reinforced this by telling them that spanking is for the good of the child. There have been numerous articles where the *Watchtower* encourages physical discipline against a child.

> Different children may need to be disciplined differently. The temperament and disposition of the individual child must be considered. One child may be very sensitive, and physical punishment, such as spanking, may not always be necessary. With another, spanking may be ineffective. Or a child may be like the servant described at proverbs 29:19, one who "will not let himself be corrected by mere words, for he understands but he is paying no heed." In such a case the child would need corporal punishment. With youngsters, temporary banishment from family

companionship can be more effective than spanking. (*Family Life,* 1978 pp. 143, 144)

Then there's this gem:

A spanking may be a lifesaver to a child, for God's word says: "Do not hold back discipline from the mere boy. In case you beat him with the rod, he will not die. With the rod, you yourself should beat him, that you may deliver his very soul from Sheol [the grave] itself." Again, "Foolishness is tied up with the heart of a boy; the rod of discipline is what will remove it far from him." (Prov. 23:13,14; 22:15) If parents hold their children's life interests dear to them, they will not weakly or carelessly let disciplinary action slip from their hands. Love will motivate them to take action, wisely and fairly, when it is needed." (*Family Life,* 1978, p. 132)

To me, these "spare the rod" Scriptures were a free pass for unlimited ass kicking and abuse in the guise of "loving discipline." By today's standards, I was physically abused because of those beatings. Yet they attempted to use God's word to substantiate their claim that corporal punishment would correct any bad behavior that I had. I can say without reservation that they were authoritarians. I was expected to do what I was told when I was told to do it or face the consequences.

The *Watchtower* (as always) chose to adjust such admonition considering modern standards as far as the rights of a child are concerned.

"Discipline primarily relates to instruction, education, and correction. It is never connected with abuse or cruelty." *Watchtower* 2014 July, 1

In addition: "The rod and reproof are what give wisdom; but a boy let on the loose will be causing his mother shame." "The rod" refers to parental authority that must be applied lovingly to prevent children from going astray. Wielding such authority does not involve abusing the child in any way. The counsel to parents is:

8

"Do not be exasperating your children, so that they do not become downhearted." (*Satisfying Life,* 2001, p. 5)

After reading the above, one can see that this is nothing but a "two Witness" rule. The changing of Scripture to conform to today's standards is more than evasive; it is a dishonest representation of the *Watchtower*'s stance on corporal punishment. First, they say beat the hell out of them, then they say show love to them; a complete double standard.

The United Nations Declaration of the Rights of the Child was adopted on November 20, 1959. Its general objective was to create a climate in which the children of the world can enjoy a safe, happy, productive, and wholesome life. At that time, it seemed that society was in denial of the abuse I was receiving and did everything opposite to this declaration. In ten carefully worded principles, the declaration affirms that all children are entitled to:

Principle 1: The child shall enjoy all the rights set forth in this Declaration. All children, without any exceptions whatsoever, shall be entitled to these rights without distinction of discrimination because of race, color, sex, language, religion, political or other opinion, national or social origin, property, birth or other status, whether of himself or of his family.

Principle 2: the child shall enjoy protection, and shall be given opportunities and facilities, by law and by other means, to enable him to develop physically, mentally, morally, spiritually and socially in a healthy and normal manner and in conditions of freedom and dignity. In the enactment of laws for this purpose the best interest of the child shall be the paramount consideration.

Principal 3: The child shall be entitled from his birth to a name and a nationality.

Principal 4: The child shall enjoy the benefits of social security. He shall be entitled to grow and develop in health, to this end special care and protection shall be provided both to him and to his mother, including

9

adequate pre-natal and post-natal care. The child shall have the right to adequate nutrition, housing, recreation and medical services.

Principal 5: The child who is physically, mentally or socially handicapped shall be given the special treatment, education and care required by his particular condition.

Principal 6: The child, for the full and harmonious development of his personality, needs love and understanding. He shall whenever possible, grow up in the care and under the responsibility of his parents, and in any case in an atmosphere of affection and of moral and material security, a child of tender years shall not, save in exceptional circumstances, be separated from his mother. Society and the public authorities shall have the duty to extend particular care to children without a family and to those without adequate means of support. Payment of state and other assistance towards the maintenance of children of large families is desirable.

Principal 7: The child is entitled to receive education, which shall be free and compulsory, at least in the elementary stages. He shall be given an education, which will promote his general culture, and enable him on a basis of equal opportunity to develop his abilities, his individual judgment, and his sense of moral and social responsibility, and to become a useful member of society. The best interest of the child shall be the guiding principle of those responsible for his education and guidance. That responsibility lies in the first place with his parents. The child shall have full opportunity for play and recreation, which should be directed to the same purposes, as education, society and the public authorities shall endeavor to promote the enjoyment of this right.

Principal 8: The child shall in all circumstances be among the first to receive protection and relief.

Principle 9: The child shall be protected against all forms of neglect, cruelty and exploitation. He shall not be the subject of traffic in any form. The child shall not be admitted to employment before an appropriate minimum age, he shall in no case be caused or permitted to engage in any occupation or employment, which would prejudice his health or education, or interfere with his physical, mental or moral development.

Principle 10: The child shall be protected from practices, which may foster racial, religious, and any other form of discrimination. He shall be brought up in a spirit of understanding, tolerance and friendship among people; also, peace and universal brotherhood in the consciousness that his energy and talents should be devoted to the service of his fellow men.

This declaration clearly states that children are not property and should not be treated as such. It states that all children require love and support. I believe my parents were in violation of many of its principles. At the time of those violations there was no outside intervention and so it was inevitable that I would become a victim of religious abuse at their hands.

The point I want to get to here is that the Jehovah's Witnesses are part of a destructive, high-control group that has cost many thousands of innocent children's lives (many that I have known) and destroyed the innocence of thousands more. Like me, it is the children who suffer the most.

Being raised as a Jehovah's Witness, there was no such thing as "life, liberty, and the pursuit of happiness" as is stated in the Declaration of Independence. Many children may face the possibility of not becoming full-fledged human beings with rights if they become a Jehovah's Witness. Since my experience, I refuse to remain silent while countless innocent children continue to suffer from being abused in the name of religion. If you are one who may be reading my story, and you are suffering any abuse by the hands of your parents or anyone else, or know someone who is at risk, you can call the Memphis Crisis Center

(Call for Kids) at 901-274-7477. Call for Kids is a hotline where trained volunteers are ready to take calls about children and youth in trouble. What kind of trouble? Just about any kind. Call if you suspect:

1. Abandonment
2. Assault
3. Beatings
4. Bullying
5. Neglect
6. Molestation
7. Self-injury
8. Runaways
9. Suicide
10. Drugs or Alcohol

# Chapter 2

# *Growing Up in the Watchtower*

As time moved on, our family began to grow and my parents started their search to find a bigger apartment or a large, single-family home. I was now ten years old and Mom was pregnant with her tenth child. We'd all had enough of each other and were tired of running into each other. At times tempers flared, where we began bickering and arguing with one another. This of course enraged Mom and Dad and led to more punishments and beatings.

In 1963 we moved to Bergen Avenue in Jersey City, New Jersey, where Mom soon gave birth. The place we moved into was an old, three-story, six-bedroom, one-and-a-half-bathroom single-family building. We had a large, scary soundproof basement where the half-bathroom was located. Our backyard was not as big as the one at our last apartment home. It was small, and facing the side of an apartment building occupied by whites only.

Earlier, our old neighbors had moved to the same location and bought the house right next door to us. At that time, the entire neighborhood was predominantly white. That's how their home became available. During the '60s, many white families didn't like the idea of living next door to a black family. So, when they moved in, many sold their homes and moved out of the community. That's how our house became available too. My parents jumped on the opportunity, and once again we became neighbors.

The first few months were just great. We had much more room than our previous home, and Dad brought home a stray dog.

At night, my brothers and I enjoyed the game of slap that face. We took joy in abusing each other physically. The game was simple; the first person who fell asleep got his face slapped by those remaining awake. My older brothers jumped on the opportunity when I fell asleep and took turns slapping the hell out of me. At times I was too scared to fall asleep, knowing that they were waiting for the opportunity. Many mornings I'd awaken with a swollen face. Sounds crazy, but it was fun; only when you weren't getting the hell slapped out of you.

The physical and emotional abuse did not stop once we left our former residence. I remember getting my first beating at our new home. One morning while in the bathroom, I had seen this peculiar thing on top of the toilet bowl. I didn't know what it was so I called some of my siblings up to view it. Suddenly, it unfolded very slowly—it was covered in blood! I couldn't figure out what it was, and no one else could either.

Mom suddenly appeared on the scene and questioned why we were in the bathroom. My siblings pointed toward the toilet, and she realized she had forgotten to throw away her used Kotex napkin. I guess out of embarrassment she became angry and chased everyone out, except for me, and proceeded in whipping my ass.

As time moved on, our home became the house of horrors. Dad did most of the whippings, which took place in the basement, where no one could hear our screams. Our basement resembled a dungeon and had a damp, funky smell to it. This is where our dog stayed most of the time, especially at night. There were about fifteen stairs leading down to the basement. The windows were very high, and had a permanent screen attached to them. When it rained, the basement got partly flooded from the rain coming in through the back basement door, leaving a damp and chilly condition. The half-bathroom was very small and only had a toilet, which was out of order. The sound of crickets, running water, bugs, and a loud, scary furnace made it just a little bit too spooky.

Most of the time when I did something wrong, this is where I would spend my detention; in the dark, sometimes for hours or the whole day. I would remain sitting at the top of the stairs in silence. The only consolation was that at times I had our dog with me. I understand that I was not always exactly an angel, but I

14

didn't deserve dungeon treatment; no one does. If a fire or something worse would have happened, I would have been trapped and unable to get out.

It seemed like I was getting whipped every other day for whatever reason; perhaps bringing home a bad report card or committing some small infraction. While he was beating me, I would make it extremely hard for him to accomplish that feat. I would either hold onto his strap or hide behind something, trying to stay out of his reach.

He also tried his hands at whipping my sisters, but to no avail. Some were bold and would not cry. Others would scream so loud it scared him half to death; that's when he left the disciplining job to my mother. As with me, she was very rough in her form when disciplining them. What I observed is that she enjoyed pulling their hair as a way of gaining control over them. She beat them with whatever she could lay her hands on. At times she was physically violent, critical, and psychologically horrifying.

During that time, I feared using use the bathroom because of my fear of mice; and we had plenty. It seems they would always come out in the middle of the night, right when I would have to take a piss. So, I came up with an idea of urinating outside of my bedroom window, located on the third floor of our home. The window was facing the alleyway, and no one could see me, so I gave it a try. As time went by, it became a habit. I got so used to doing it that it skipped my mind that water freezes, and since winter had just arrived, my urine never reached the ground; it froze onto the side of the house. It produced a yellow urine icicle that was certainly an eyesore and was sure to be noticed by someone.

One day Dad ventured into the alleyway and noticed the frozen piss-cicles and was extremely pissed himself. Seems he knew exactly who did it. Once again, I had a date with his leather belt. I thought my act was a mere peccadillo but got beaten as though it was a hideous crime; regardless, I still wasn't going to use the bathroom at night. I had to come up with another idea.

Since I shared the same bed with one of my younger brothers, I thought I could exploit his weakness of bed-wetting. He would wet the bed mostly every night and Dad was aware of this. He was my way out. Since we both shared the same bed, the simple solution was to urinate on his side of the bed and he would take the blame. After seeing him get punished so many times, I felt sorry for him and found another way to unload my urine. From now on when I got the urge, I would urinate in jars and then empty them in the morning, saving my brother from frequent ass whippings *and* my adventures with mice.

Growing up in the *Watchtower* was like growing up in a tiny Western town, a million miles from nowhere, with nothing to do. Everything fun to do was always bad. There were no cousins to play with and as mentioned, we couldn't have any "worldly" friends. It was like being a POW. Even when I did manage to get out I had no idea how to interact with other people my age, as my parents never invited any around to play or socialize and I was not allowed to go to their homes. All they had me do was preach, preach, and preach.

During these years, my home life continued to be drab and a drag, mainly because of being isolated. For instance, everything we did, we did as a family, minus cousins, uncles, aunts, or grandparents. My only friends were Jehovah's Witnesses, and they were just as dull as I was.

My view of the world was limited to the four walls of our home. During the sixties, they were having riots right across the bridge in Newark, New Jersey, and I knew nothing of it. I was forced to stay inside most of the time. I most certainly didn't have any knowledge of major events in black history, or black history in general. Sadly, I didn't have a clue who Martin Luther King Jr. was until my later years. What I didn't know is that I was being set up for social ostracism. Isolation was used to prevent me from having a well-developed sense of reality about life.

During those years, I did find time to create some excitement for myself if I could get away with it. My greatest adventures began during Halloween. Since we didn't celebrate the occasion, I didn't have a Halloween costume, but that didn't stop me. I simply poked a few holes in a large brown paper bag and covered my head, using it as my mask. As I ventured from door to door, I collected loads of candy and enjoyed the moment.

Catching spiders was another great adventure; something that drove my mother crazy. My fascination for spiders led me to catch them, feed them (flies), and mate them in jars collected from her pantry. All in all, I had at least ten jars of spiders, both large and small.

I do believe that Dad sensed that many of us were getting bored and at times we headed out to various parks. During those outings, we would start off by having a Bible study, which included studying the *Watchtower* magazine. It was quite boring, and it seemed like it would take hours before it was over with. We spent more time studying than playing like normal kids do.

As time moved on and Mom continue to give birth, food was getting scarce. Dad continued to do whatever he could to compensate for this, including raiding the garbage bin of local restaurants daily. Whatever food items the restaurant would discard at the end of the day, he would collect them, if they were edible. No matter how he tried to compensate, I continued to have hunger pangs and needed to curb my appetite, so once again I turned into a food bandit.

Now that I was much older, I became more sophisticated in my approach and had help from one of my brothers. We banded together many nights and raided the kitchen refrigerator. It was a little easier than on Randolph Avenue because our parents' bedroom was in front of the house on the second floor. The kitchen was downstairs. All we needed to do was bypass the squeaky stairs, and we were home free. Mom also had a freezer located in the basement where she kept her frozen food. There was frozen bologna (my favorite), frankfurters, cheese, etc. basically, anything she could freeze.

The best time to steal frozen food was during the winter months. By then the heat would be on and the radiator in my room, which gave off tremendous heat, would be perfect for thawing frozen food. It took Mom a while to notice the missing

17

food and when she did, she put a padlock on the refrigerator. What was I to do now? I thought. Everything was locked up; all but the dried food. That, of course, was my last option and next target.

Hominy grits in a tall glass was the order of the day. With this, I wouldn't have to get up in the middle of the night to steal anything. Before bedtime, I would simply pour grits in a glass, add some hot sink water, add sugar and milk, place it under my bed, and in a few hours, it would be ready to consume. But it didn't help that much because I remained hungry during the early night hours.

Dad started giving us allowances for the first time and that would help some. I would always get fifty cents and spent it mostly on candy. In those days, you could buy a lot of candy for that amount. While going from door to door selling *Watchtower*, and *Awake!* magazines and books, and I kept most of the money from that. It made me start enjoying going from door to door and eventually I stopped being a food bandit.

Even though that period came to an end, I was still accused of wrongdoing if something was missing. For example, Mom used to leave food on the kitchen table for Dad when he came home for lunch in the early afternoon. At times, I would come home from school on my lunch break almost the same time that he arrived. Most of the time, Mom was not home when we arrived. She was either out shopping or in field service.

One afternoon he arrived earlier than I, ate his food, and went back to work. When I arrived, I had no idea that he had been there. After eating my lunch, I was ready to head back to school when she arrived. She had asked me if I had seen him. I replied no. She wanted to know what happened to the food she left for him. I had no idea what she was talking about; I simply didn't know, as I explained to her. She immediately became enraged, started yelling at me, saying that she was tired of me lying, and was going to beat the truth out of me.

At that time my older sister arrived, and wanted to know what was going on and why Mom was so upset. While explaining the situation, she got ahold of a curtain rod, ordered me to take

my shirt off and started striking me across the back with it. My
older sister just stood and watched, and seemed to enjoy seeing
me get punished. The beating hurt so bad, I confessed to
everything to get her to stop the punishment. That early afternoon
I wore many stripes and welt marks across my back.

I wasn't permitted to return to school that afternoon because
of the visible marks left on me; perhaps she thought I would tell
my teacher. I was then locked in the basement until later that
evening. Once let out I was hungry, hurting, and scared. I feared
for myself because I didn't know if she would tell Dad once he
returned home from work. If so that would mean another ass
kicking, so I hid in my room until it was time for supper.

As I sat down to eat he entered the kitchen and came straight
towards me. I just about pissed my pants. As I sat there, scared
beyond belief, he reached into his pocket and gave me my
allowance. As I was thanking him Mom interjected, saying I
didn't deserve anything, informing him that I had stolen his lunch
earlier that afternoon. He disagreed, saying that he had eaten it
earlier before I came home from school. My older sister, who
witnessed the beating, pulled off my shirt, showing him the welts
on my back. I wished he would say something on my behalf but
he said nothing and just walked away. His lack of protection said
a lot about what was in store for me while being raised a
Jehovah's Witness.

# Chapter 3

# *My School Years*

From the start, childhood was a compendium of school days, some truly inspiring, some to be endured, some a refuge from reality and fears. It was very hard to compete with the other children because there were too many obstacles in the way. For example, in our classroom, it was customary every morning for us to pledge allegiance to the American flag. At times, we would have assemblies where grades one through eight would gather to make the pledge and sing the national anthem. When we were told to stand and place our right hand over our heart, I would stand with my hands remaining at my side. During the national anthem, I would sit and remain in mute mode. All the other kids would look at me in a weird way. I was questioned by my teacher as to why I wouldn't participate in the activities. In response, I told them that my parents instructed me not to salute the flag or participate in the singing of the national anthem because they were Jehovah's Witnesses. Once they were made aware of this, I was surprised that my educators were not aware that I was being mentally abused at home and that I was under cult influence.

During that time, there were a lot of events taking place in the world; the Cold War, missiles in Cuba, Vietnam, etc.; and here I was, telling them I couldn't salute the flag. Perhaps they thought my parents were communists. After that moment, I felt that I was always being watched by everyone on assembly day to see if I was going to salute the flag. The pressure was so great that at times I partially saluted the flag by raising my right hand halfway up my, chest then lowering it when no one was looking. At times, I didn't sit for the national anthem and acted as though I was singing along with the other students by lip syncing. At least that took some of the pressure off. I still dreaded when we

20

had school assemblies. At times, I faked as if I was sick and got sent to the nurse just to get out of it.

The pressure was on again when the holidays came. I couldn't participate in any of the activities surrounding them; especially the Christmas holiday activities, which were filled with excitement. I was also barred from other activities, such as school clubs, school dances, school plays, many school songs, the Boy Scouts or other calendar holiday activities.

I always found myself sitting in the classroom alone while those activities were taking place. The teachers would give me class assignments to pass the time. It was as though I was being punished because of my parents' religious beliefs. The other students passing by in the corridor looked at me in a strange way, as if something was wrong with me. There was also a lot of bullying associated with this as well. I was bullied because I had to face many of them when I went preaching from door to door, which was embarrassing. They harassed me the next day at school, calling me a punk, along with other not so very pleasant names.

All in all, my parents were saying one thing (with God/Armageddon in the background) and the teachers and classmates were saying another (patriotism/love for God and country.) It introduced a lot of inconsistency and confusion into my life. School was going to be a juggling act no matter what.

The fact remains that once mentioning that my parents were Jehovah's Witnesses the heat was on, and I found it hard to concentrate on my schoolwork, and my grades suffered. During those years, I was an under-achiever, never striving hard for good grades. At school, I had underwater marks—below C level.

I loved to learn but found it hard to integrate into a school system that was flawed according to what I was being taught at home.

I spent eleven years in grammar school. During that time, it seemed like I was one of the oldest students in the class. In fact, I was in one class so long, the other pupils used to bring me apples thinking I was the teacher. (A little humor to break the monotony.) Whenever I got my report card, my promotion was always in danger. I was a good student but the teachers always gave me a P (poor) in behavior. I believe it was because I didn't salute the flag and sat for the national anthem. I failed in math, English, and only did well in science; I loved science projects.

My parents had to sign my report card before I could bring it back to school, so there was no way around not showing it to them. Once viewed, the first thing they would look for is what mark I got in behavior. As mentioned, it always said poor and the whippings continued. When I failed the seventh grade, I was so petrified that my world was going to come to an end if my parents found out that I set my report card afire in a desk drawer. In doing so, I could have burned the whole school down. I'm only happy that it was a small fire and no one got hurt as the fire department extinguished the blaze.

After my parents found out there was a fire at the school, they fell for my story about not getting my report card and I was spared an ass kicking. The saddest part about that is that I had to repeat the seventh grade.

They had a summer program called summer school where you could make up the grades and go on to the next grade when school started, but I would rather stay back a grade than be punished the entire summer vacation; I had been through that before when I got left back in the fifth grade.

While navigating through this period I was socially awkward, like many Jehovah's Witness kids I knew. I was not allowed to participate in normal acts of citizenship with anyone who wanted to be my friend because they were "worldly" people and would die soon.

One of the most discouraging aspects I experienced was not being able to use my athletic ability. I was always interested in playing baseball but that was certainly out of bounds, per my parents. I once had a dream that I would one day join the Little League baseball team and perhaps once grown, become a professional baseball player. Then again, it was only a dream.

According to the *Watchtower* society, playing competitive sports was bad because it involved idol worship. It also meant not being spiritual.

Once graduating from grammar school (beard and all), entering high school was like entering the twilight zone. For example, I had no career plans; no interest in SAT prep and submitting college applications. Community, technical, or junior college were forbidden by the *Watchtower* society. So therefore, to me, further education was a waste of time.

I can still remember the ridiculous *Watchtower* articles encouraging my parents to keep me out of worldly "educational" activities; complete nonsense.

Parents who are Jehovah's Witnesses have another very sound reason for channeling their children's lives into useful trades. They know from fulfilled Bible prophecy that today's industrial society is near its end. Soon it will be given its death stroke by Almighty God himself. After that, in God's new order a reconstruction work will be done to transform this entire earth into a paradise. Trades of many types will be very useful then, as will skills in agriculture and homemaking. So, by guiding their children away from the so called 'higher' education of today, these parents spare their children exposure to an increasingly demoralizing atmosphere, and at the same time prepare them for life in a new system as well. (*Awake!* June 8, 1967)

Then this one:

The influence and spirit of this world is to get ahead, to make a name for oneself. Many schools now have student counselors who encourage one to pursue higher education after high school, to pursue a career with a future in this system of things. Do not be influenced by them. Do not let them "brainwash" you with the Devil's propaganda to get ahead, to make something of yourself

23

in this world. This world has very little time left! Any 'future' this world offers is no future!

If you are a young person, you also need to face the fact that you will never grow old in this present system of things. Why not? Because all evidence in fulfillment of Bible prophecy indicates that this corrupt system is due to end in a few years. Of the generation that observed the beginning of the "last days" in 1914. Jesus foretold: 'This generation will by no means pass away until all these things occur.' (Matt. 24:34). Therefore, as a young person you will never fulfill any career that this system offers. If you are in high school and thinking about a college education, it means four, perhaps even six or eight years to graduate into a specialized career. But where will this system of things be by that time? It will be well on the way toward its finish, if not actually gone! (*Awake!* May 22, 1969, p. 15)

The above is simply hogwash and absurd! I think I could have been a better student if I had parents who were devoted to the development of my mind rather than cramming it with extraneous *Watchtower* matters that had no bearing on the tasks that lay before me in life. Unfortunately, however, I was not that much an avid reader or student, and it became obvious that a high school diploma was not in my future. For lack of intelligent guidance, then, I asked Dad to sign me out of school and without hesitation, he obliged. This would be the start of the end for me. Unfortunately, it also meant that I wasn't going to plan my adulthood very well. Said the late legendary UCLA coach John Wooden: "Failure to prepare is preparing to fail."

# Chapter 4

## *Kicking the Habit*

My mind was now set on getting baptized and becoming a Jehovah's Witness. With the subject of Armageddon constantly being brought up, I most certainly didn't want to be killed by Jehovah. There were a few reasons why I continued to contemplate this; first, I wanted to change the way my parents felt about me, and secondly and mostly, I felt guilty about engaging in the sin of masturbation.

I began doing this when I picked the habit up from one of my older brothers I shared a bedroom with. He was jacking off every night while looking at a magazine. Out of curiosity, I asked him what he was reading and doing. After explaining what masturbation was, he then explained the method and what the payoff would be. After trying it a few times, I didn't achieve a thing, only because I didn't know what to expect or what the hell he was talking about. When I did get it right; wow, the feeling resembled an erupting volcano with full force. I also took an interest in viewing girly magazines, which brought on even more excitement while jacking off.

Whenever we gathered for our daily Bible study at home, I couldn't wait for its conclusion so I could engage in viewing my porn material. By then I had a large collection, well hidden from my father. He was always snooping around in our bedroom and I believe he had a sixth sense for this, so I had to find a good hiding place. I remember one Bible study we had (which took forever) in which he had instructed us earlier to remember the names of some biblical men in the Bible called Shadrach, Meshach, and Abednego. He had asked me what role they played in the Bible and because I didn't remember, I was severely punished. The truth of the matter is that I couldn't have cared less about who they were. The only thing on my mind was masturbating.

Since my brother and I shared the same room, unlike him, I felt embarrassed about masturbating in front of him, or for that matter, being caught by my parents, so I became a closet masturbator. The only problem I had with that was that I couldn't see my girly magazines in the dark. I got to love it so much that I didn't care if I got my ass kicked by my parents anymore. In fact, I wouldn't even cry when being whipped because I had something else to fall back on, in my mind. Randy was my name and masturbating was my game.

I became so horny I even used our vacuum cleaner from time to time to get a stronger feeling at payoff time. I only stopped using it because I was afraid of being castrated because the suction was too strong. From time to time I became more sophisticated in my jerking off methods that weren't as dangerous. Using my hand was safer but got boring at times. Being right-handed, I often tried using my left hand, which seemed to be a mission impossible. It wouldn't perform like my right hand because for some reason I had to stroke harder, which made my hand swell.

However, during my jerk-off adventures, I was constantly being taught that the atmosphere in the field of masturbation was not conducive to practicing the "truth" and it would result in loss of Jehovah's approval. In the '70s, the Witnesses had a book called the youth book that said:

The real question, then, is, not how much physical harm could result from masturbation, but whether spiritual harm results…to help to avoid or reduce sexual tension…you may find it helpful to sleep on your side rather than on your back or face down. Another thing that may be helpful is to see to it that your clothing does not unnecessarily cause friction with the sexual organs…In fact, masturbation can lead into homosexuality…Contrary to what many persons think, homosexuals are not born that way, but their homosexual behavior, is learned." (*Your Youth: Getting the Best Out of It*, pp 35:42)

Masturbation may cause homosexuality? Heck, I never knew what that word meant. All I knew is that I was "spiritually weak" and started praying for help daily; that's when everything went wrong.

One Sunday afternoon, I took the time out to pray out loud to Jehovah, making a vow that I would always be faithful to him, and asked him to help me conquer the habit of masturbation and to help me find a job. That's when one of my sisters overheard the conversation. She wanted to know who I was talking to and what I was talking about. I simply told her to mind her own business. She immediately called Mom and told her that I was disrespecting her by talking back. Mom became angry and punched me in the mouth, busting my lip. Blood was everywhere and becoming enraged I lifted her up, pinning her up against the wall. She screamed out to Dad and he came to her assistance, pulling me away from her. He picked me up, put me over his shoulder, and carried me down to the basement. I expected at least to be killed, but he did nothing of the kind. He locked me in the basement and kept me there until things cooled off. I was somewhat timid after being let out because I still had to face Mom, and became nauseated after thinking what she would do to me later. That's when I decided to run away from home.

The physical, mental, and emotional cruelty became very wearing and I needed to get away fast. Her punching in the mouth was the last punishment I was going to take. For now, the thought of being baptized would have to wait. It was time to get off the fence, and quickly.

Shortly before I left home, I contacted one of my older brothers. Earlier, Dad had thrown him out because he was in a heavy relationship with a "worldly" girl, which was against his rules. She had a small apartment and took him in, and was kind enough to accept me after I told her what had happened at home. As I cowered in their apartment, not knowing what to do next, Dad came looking for me. Once finding out where my brother lived, he paid him a visit, hoping to find me there. As he spoke with him, I was hiding in the bedroom closet, frightened half to death at the thought that he would find me and return me home for the greatest ass whipping of all time. My brother convinced him that he hadn't seen me and soon he was on his way. I couldn't wait to exhale.

The next day, my brother convinced me that the best place for me was home, and he didn't want Dad visiting him after being thrown out himself. I disagreed at first, but realized that I had no job and no money, so I complied. I was freaked out about returning and facing the consequences of running away; nevertheless, I returned home, unwitting of what was in store for me.

Once returning, I was happy that my parents weren't at home. It took away some of the fear that I was carrying within. He was at work, and she was in field service. My siblings were happy to see me, as I was happy to see them, and we all gave each other a hug. My next step was to go to my room, where I cowered until my parents' return. My siblings would break the news to them that I had returned home. I didn't know what thoughts they were entertaining after being told, but knew they would come after me sooner or later; it was only a matter of time. I could only expect the best and get ready for the worst.

For some strange reason, I received no punishment at all. In fact, they said nothing to me for the next few days. That made it more frightening because I didn't know what to expect or what they were thinking. Since Dad was at work most of the time I didn't have to deal with him, and tried to stay away from Mom as much as possible. Every day I headed out looking for work and once returning, cowered in my room, staying out of harm's way until dinnertime. Even that was a scary moment because I was sitting face-to-face with them and terrified because they said nothing. In my heart, I knew that all hell was going to break loose at any moment; and then, just like that, it happened.

One Saturday morning while eating breakfast, Mom made Dad aware that I didn't clean the backyard up as instructed. He then asked me why, to which I responded that I had forgotten. I assured him that I would complete it as soon as I finished eating; "But right now, I'm eating." Why did I say that? This would be his opportunity to get even with me for running away and I was right. With great anger, he said, "Oh, you think you're a man now?" With all his might, he yanked me away from the table, wrestled me to the floor and started striking me. I resisted a little but was no match for him. My siblings began screaming at him, telling him to leave me alone, but to no avail. Mom just stood there, gazing on the scene with an air of heartless satisfaction. I wasn't surprised by what happened; I expected the big payback for running away.

After that incident, I remained in my room most of the time, thinking about baptism and what the future would hold for me.

# Chapter 5

# *The Narcissistic Puppet Master*

Families that get along and operate well together are credited to the matriarch or patriarch. Therefore, when a family doesn't run smoothly, it is because the matriarch or patriarch is not doing what is necessary to keep the family mentally and emotionally healthy. It's like running a business. If the manager does a poor job, the business will suffer and fail. If the manager does a good job, the business will thrive and succeed. Good managers/leaders are very important to the health and well-being of a family and a business, and if you are not healthy and well yourself, then you cannot be a good manager of others.

My father's (the patriarch) job was supposed to be about bringing everyone together without prejudice, but with love. Yet to speak truthfully of him would be to say that he is a man in whose heart the quality of kindness or of justice is not found. A rough, rude person, united with an uncultivated mind and an avaricious spirit are his prominent characteristics. This is the life he has chosen with this new religion. He has been deeply brainwashed by repetitive studies and brainwashed association. It's nearly impossible for him to break out of that mind-set because he is a narcissist.

At the Kingdom Hall, he been appointed as a ministerial servant. "Servants" are the assistants to the congregation elders. I would liken his role to that of a deacon. In the *Watchtower* society there are a host of positions, such as, special pioneers, Gilead missionaries, Bethelites, ministerial servants, sound, maintenance, microphones, literature, circuit overseer, district overseer, assembly overseers, and as mentioned, elders. The elder position is one of the lowest (non-paid) positions of power in the *Watchtower* society, and he had his eyes set on that. Sooner or later he would land the position and become more of a tyrant than he was as a ministerial servant.

He was also an egomaniac. He loved the stage, and used it to get attention. He wanted to be, and had to be, in the spotlight, no matter what. For example, if he was scheduled to give a talk (another word for sermon) and he became aware that his house was on fire and burning down, it wouldn't matter to him, he would continue with his talk. His egotism was no different than the rest of the black male Jehovah's Witness speakers I was raised around; a plain case of mistaken nonentity.

I recall one Friday evening, he was schedule to give a talk and at the very moment he approached the podium, I developed a sharp pain on the right side of my body. The pain was so bad I couldn't walk. As I withered in pain, I was carried to the rear of the Kingdom Hall, where elders and some members removed my upper garments to find out what was going on. Dad viewed the entire episode from the podium but seemed to not care less. Because of his ego, he continued with his sermon. Not to mention, Mom never signaled him to get his ass off the stage and take me to the hospital. They simply ignored my suffering until the pain subsided.

What I learned in that situation is that for him to be an elder (and take the stage), he had to control everything; even his emotions toward his immediate family. If he didn't, he would not have exemplary privileges in the congregation. As mentioned, he was in a real hurry to reach out for responsibilities in the congregation at any expense. Most of the "real" responsibility that a father holds for his family had been put aside to serve the *Watchtower* society. From the very start they used him and made him believe that it was all about them and nothing about us.

During that time, I never realized that in the real stage of life he was void of a platform, so he joined the organization to attract an audience over which he expounded on their views. The *Watchtower* society provided the soap-box opportunity for him to get special attention, to rule others via religious doctrine. There, he would never have to finish his education to better himself or provide a future for our family, and it wasn't a requirement.

On the outside, he painted himself as the picture of a perfect Jehovah's Witness, but behind closed doors and out of sight of fellow worshipers, he created a hell-home for his children. He was almost fanatical in his pursuit of advancement in the organization. This became more toxic as he tried harder to reinforce the mandate by the *Watchtower*. Everyone was expected to toe the line and support him in his theocratic progression to eldership. He began to show judgmental attitudes toward me and developed a haughty attitude about my own self-worth as a young publisher. He didn't care one bit about my feelings; he was an apathetic, autocratic, obdurate, and an egocentrically obtuse man. There was constant censorship of any correspondence with family and friends. He denounced all non-witness relatives as "doomed" human beings, and in the process, avoided all family functions, including religious worship. It's only sad that I never attended service with my grandparents and they never attended meetings at the Kingdom Hall. As time moved on, he became cliquish and "holier than thou."

When it came down to my mother, she showed deference to him. That was the role of a Jehovah's Witness wife. In the *Watchtower* literature, it told her that her role was a role of submission, exclusion, and a silent partner. Even while at the Kingdom Hall she had no rights. She could give parts in the Theocratic Ministry School or participate in demonstrations in the Service Meeting, but she was not allowed to give talks, instructions from the platform, give prayer or become an elder. Jehovah's Witness ministers' wives were strictly prohibited from having a livelihood because it would interfere with the duties of her husband and would bring disgrace to the organization. To me, Dad always treated her as a lowly servant confined to the ghetto (for life), unable to display her real talents, whatever they were. If she raised her voice or objected to the organization's rules, he would immediately reprimand her with certain Bible Scriptures. I believe he drove her crazy with his passive, non-reactive style and disinterest in her feelings.

A narcissistic husband has two requirements; to manipulate, and control, just like a puppet master. He had been pulling her strings for a long time, controlling what went on beneath her. His interactions with her were almost always beneficial to him. He was one who was in control of himself and controlled the outcome of any situation. Most of the time, he forced her to mimic his own actions. He prevented her from acting with gestures or movements of her own. He paralyzed her mind and forced her into not using her God-given ability to love her children 100 percent.

Much of his interpersonal aggression towards her was observed by me since I was a young child, as mentioned. Observing how things work when one is bossed and bullied represents the expression of an extremely important stage in the development of a personality and self-esteem. Her most powerful urges to be successful as an entrepreneur had been laid to rest because she was limited and regulated by him. If she was to realize her own potential, one of her first prerequisites would be an understanding of what that potential is.

What stood between her and her potential was her puppet master Jehovah's Witness husband. Around people he was quiet and totally placid in his private life; a man who never raised his voice at home when surrounded by visitors. He managed to project such an impressive image. It was equality dressed in a lamb's outfit when in fact it was a wolf.

***

As with most Jehovah's Witness fathers, he is the most plastic, the most uneducable, the most manipulative man there ever was. He is both an autocrat and the most complicated organism of all social beings. He could not bear the idea that she should ever have a life of her own. So, she had to be maintained, with the minimum gift of himself, inside his orbit and not outside. She is restricted in her sphere to small things, and with these she becomes satisfied.

Under his leadership, she has been made to despise her own possibilities, yet the fault here is not inherently hers, but in what

33

she has been taught about herself as a woman. The following is a recording of a public talk by Samuel Herd, who later went on to become a member of the governing body of Jehovah's Witnesses. He makes the following comments about why women need to be in subjection to men.

> You know, scientists say that the cranial capacity of a woman is 10% smaller than that of a man so now this shows that she's just not equipped for the role of headship. Her role is one of subjection to the man. Her role is that of submissiveness and that means that she should recognize that she is a woman and be glad to be a woman. Never want to be what you are not equipped to be. ... Sometimes we hear her say, oh if-if-if-if I-I were a man I'd do this and I'd do that, as if to be wishing to be something that she is not designed to be. Do you know what that borders on? That borders on homosexuality. And do you know what the devil is doing nowadays? He's taking women who want to be men and makes men out of them.
>
> Cooperate, and never compete; you would recognize if you truly loved your husband, you are not equipped mentally, emotionally, physically, or somatically for the role of competition. You would never pit your mind against his. She'll work extremely hard never to show that she's quicker in mind than her husband.

(www.youtubesamuelherdtalk;womenhavesmallbrains)

After watching this video I asked myself, what kind of woman stands by such a man? My hypothesis is: caring too much about what others think and pinning one's self-esteem on the opinions of others is, indeed, a weakness and a vulnerability.

This ignorant, uneducated fool trying to pontificate on what he knows nothing about only proves how backwards and misogynistic the Jehovah's Witness leaders are. Yet when all has been said and done, people like my mother accept this kind of rubbish. If she was strong enough to open her eyes and face reality, she would see the machinations of a psychopathic husband, a narcissist. But she has been weak and unable to escape from his hold. She has been influenced by his power. He remains a self-seeking, self-righteous individual; having no respect for others or for the dignity of their lives in general. The idea of a person's inability to love cannot be summarized better than by quoting Paracelsus:

> He, who knows nothing, loves nothing. He who can do nothing understands nothing. He who understands nothing is worthless. But he who understands also loves, notices, sees...The more knowledge is inherent in a thing, the greater the love...Anyone who imagines that all fruit ripen at the same time as the strawberries knows nothing about grapes.

## Dad and Money

When it came down to money or financial situations, he never discussed anything. Never taught the importance of life insurance policies, investments in stocks, bonds, treasury bills, or municipal funds. Never taught how to turn a nickel into a dime, or a dime into a dollar. Never obligated himself to build generational wealth for his family.

The truth of the matter is, he got away from his financial obligation for his family, as many Jehovah Witness fathers do. I always asked myself, how he could let a so-called religion instruct him to do this to his family? Instruct him to be non-supportive and basically selfish? Now that he was a full-fledged Jehovah's Witness, they constantly pushed him to bring the rest of the family aboard the *Watchtower* wagon.

# Chapter 6

# *"In the Truth"*

During my teen years, we continued having weekly home Bible studies. In the past, we were being taught out of a book called *The Paradise Book*; now we were being taught out of a book called the *Truth Book*, replete with Kingdom songs and prayers. All aspects of Jehovah's Witness life were dictated by that book. It outlined the basis of the faith and helped to define what it meant to be a Jehovah's Witness. Being much older now, I began to understand what was being taught by the Jehovah's Witnesses.

I was enticed by the illustrations of paradise, endless beauty, forever young, all while hugging lions and tigers, which seemed fascinating to me at that time. It wouldn't be long before we were attending regular meetings at the local Kingdom Hall. It was in a very poor (ghetto) residential neighborhood, within walking distance from our home. There were three meetings a week, conducted at three different times. On Wednesdays, we had the book study for one hour. This meeting was a question-and-answer discussion of a *Watchtower* Bible and Tract Society publication, along with the Bible. The book study was held at a Jehovah's Witness's private home that was located three blocks from our house.

On Fridays, two meetings were held. First was the Theocratic Ministry School, followed by the Service Meeting. The school involved both training courses and student deliveries on a variety of topics, with the focus on making everyone a more capable minister and public speaker. The Service Meeting had three parts. First were the announcements, when congregation matters were discussed, or the all-important dis-fellowshipped or ex-communications were announced. After the announcements were two parts covering how to be more effective in the door-to-door ministry. We were taught how to overcome people's objections and to hopefully be persuasive enough to start a Bible study with them.

On Sunday, we had a two-hour meeting that began with the public talk and concluded with the *Watchtower* study, a question-and-answer consideration of the magazine of the same name that the Jehovah's Witnesses are known for. If I didn't raise my hand to be called on to answer any questions given, I would be castigated by my parents once home. To them that was a sign that I didn't study my lesson.

Dad had a system of punishments for such infractions; either a whipping or going to bed without supper. Unconscionably, before being whipped, he always read a Jehovah's Witness Scripture as justification for the physical abuse (foolishness tied up with the heart of a boy and the rod of discipline is what will remove it far from him); upon which basis he used to beat the living crap out of me. To counter this, I would always raise my hand (at least halfway) when a question was asked, hoping I wouldn't be called upon; anything to keep him from kicking my ass.

Usually my parents sat behind me. I couldn't move, nod, chew gum, or talk...not unless I wanted to get slapped upside my head in front of everyone. The meetings were very dull, quiet, and resembled a funeral home wake. Even the scheduled speakers were boring; many so boring and dull, they couldn't even entertain a doubt. I clearly remember one older white elder. When he spoke, he was hither, thither, and yawn, and was responsible for me getting slapped upside the head for nodding off whenever he gave a sermon. Most of the Jehovah's Witness elders I heard were boring to a point—the point of departure.

When it was time to praise the Lord in song, simply put, the Jehovah's Witnesses do not believe in choirs. They have their own brand of hymns to separate themselves from Christendom. When singing Witness songs, we simply stood and sang songs out of a *Watchtower* song book, which was equally boring.

During my youth, my dad did everything in the attempt to make sure that I was bending to the Jehovah's Witness stick. It did figure heavily in my young life. As far back as I could ascertain, he used certain methods to control my mind, control my behavior, control my thoughts, control the information I received, and control my emotions. He sincerely believed that the *Watchtower* society was "the truth" and had the only answers to life's problems

Once I was enrolled in the Theocratic Ministry School, I would routinely be given five-minute speaking assignments at congregation meetings, then critiqued by an elder if any mistakes were made in my presentation. This was done in front of a mostly adult audience. Most churches have Sunday school for their youth and separate them from the adults. It's just the opposite with the *Watchtower* society; everyone's crammed together. You're immediately injected with older adults and must perform on their level. You must act like them, talk like them, walk like them, and think like them.

In those days, I spent my time going to meetings, district assemblies, proselytizing for the organization, and found myself doing manual labor for them free of charge. My siblings and I was assigned to clean the local Kingdom Hall every other weekend. The duties included washing windows, dusting blinds, mopping floors, vacuuming carpet, and sanitizing bathrooms. Not only did we clean the place, we painted it and made repairs to it. Without any remuneration, we also cleaned up after circuit assemblies and district assemblies.

During that time, I worked in the trucking department unloading food, and worked on the food line serving food. I also worked in the garbage department collecting garbage. I remember those days, moving up and down the corridors with huge garbage dumpsters, collecting trash. At that time, I enjoyed what I was doing because I felt it was a service to Jehovah. This was also in line with the organization's motto of keeping costs down by using "volunteer" workers.

In our family, there was very little money. Dad had ten hungry mouths to feed with a very small salary and a severely stretched budget. Mom had soon given birth to another child. She was now thirty-five years old with eleven children. Now the task in providing for us became even harder. I always kept a low profile because Dad seemed to be a little stressed, so I didn't want to tick him off with any rules broken. As he struggled to maintain our family, he came up with a few ideas to fill the void; we became garbage pickers.

During the early morning hours, my brothers and I would venture out with him to find whatever we could that we could trade in for money at the recycle center for whatever it was worth. We collected newspapers, copper, brass, etc. We made more money collecting newspapers and magazines than anything else.

The week before Christmas was very important to me. It was the best time to pick garbage because our neighbors would throw out old toys and other items. Since we didn't celebrate Christmas, it would be our best chance to get things. I remember finding an old bicycle on my first Christmas garbage pick. It was in good shape except that it needed a few repairs; nevertheless, I was happy.

Besides picking garbage, I found other ways of making money to help with our family's financial problems. During the winter, I got permission to shovel snow for money. In my first outing I made twenty-five dollars, the most money I ever had in my life. I was excited thinking about all the candy I would buy, but then came back to reality knowing I would have to give a third of those earnings to Dad.

During the summer season, I made extra money trimming my neighbors' hedges and mowing their lawns. As mentioned, Dad wanted a third of everything I made, so there was not much left after giving him his cut. At times, I lied about how much money I made, just to keep some extra bucks in my pockets. All in all, the extra money being brought in paid off in keeping a roof over our heads and food in our stomachs. But if there was anything I loved about working and making money, it was this; I enjoyed being out of the house, even if only for a couple of hours.

At least I wouldn't be in my parents' line of fire and wouldn't have to worry about getting whipped or beat.

During the weekend, we were required to go from door to door to peddle the *Watchtower*'s message in the ghetto. There was no getting out of that. Through the rain, wind, sleet, and snow, my siblings and I would preach in poverty-stricken neighborhoods surrounded by filth, scarcity, dilapidated houses, deteriorating and squalid slums, to find new converts.

Every weekend I witnessed the concentration of poor people living literally and figuratively atop one another along with the proliferation of trash. Most projects had twelve floors and were surrounded by the smell of feces and urine (especially in the elevators). Our territory card read "South Unit," the poorest neighborhoods in Jersey City, New Jersey.

Very rarely were we sent to the affluent white community in neighboring Bayonne. When sent there, we ran into many whites who felt we didn't belong in their community and didn't mind letting us know about it. When we came knocking at 8:00 a.m., they were furious. I can remember knocking on a white homeowner's door early one Sunday morning and asking him if he would like to live forever in paradise. He was furious, saying in return, no, but would you like to die right now?

Being able to knock on doors (no matter what time) and wake some poor dude up out of his hangover on a cold Saturday morning, or disturb some old man trying to get it up after trying all night to make love to his wife, to talk about religion, was no small feat. All in all, I was happy that we were relegated to proselytizing in the ghetto. Not meaning romanticizing it as a bastion of salt-of-the-earth authenticity; yes, conditions were appalling, and seemed to be run-down and defeated. But black people were a little bit kinder than whites in their affluent communities.

During this time, the thought of baptism crossed my mind once again. The conviction that Armageddon was "just around the corner" was one of the few tenets that I pondered in helping me make that decision. First and not least, I wanted to maintain a state of well-being with my parents. If they were happy with

40

me getting baptized, then perhaps I would receive more positive attention; and secondly, I was coming close to conquering the habit of masturbation. If I could kick the habit, then I would be ready. That wouldn't take long because at this stage in my life, I had developed a superiority complex over the rest of society as I was taught to do. I firmly believed that the Jehovah's Witnesses were a step above the rest with Jehovah God, and was comforted in the thought that he would make things right, even if it meant destroying these obstinate non-believers at Armageddon.

Once ready, I informed my parents of my decision. They were in total agreement, and arranged a Bible study for me with a Jehovah's Witness elder. This is one of the rules of the *Watchtower* society before one is indoctrinated. Before being baptized there were a host of questions I had to answer correctly. The two outstanding questions asked at the time of baptism were:

(1) Have you recognized yourself as a sinner and needing salvation from Jehovah God? And have you acknowledged that this salvation proceeds from him and through his Ransomer, Christ Jesus?

(2) On the basis of this faith in God and in his provision for redemption, have you dedicated yourself unreservedly to Jehovah God to do his will henceforth as that will is revealed to you through Christ Jesus and through God's Word as his Holy Spirit makes plain?

I answered yes to these two questions and now qualified for baptism. The elders and others present witnessed my affirmation of dedication. I was then appropriately baptized and officially in the "truth" a full-fledged Jehovah's Witness.

From that time on, great changes came over my life. Up until then I'd had a loveless relationship with both parents. Getting baptized seemed to please them and my relationship with them got somewhat better, but I was still under the microscope. In fact, I was seldom happy afterwards because I was regulated in everything I wanted to do. As time moved on and I became more

41

regulated than ever, I always asked myself, why in the world did I get baptized? The truth of the matter is that I had not yet developed critical thinking skills, but still, I didn't want to second guess myself. Being in the "truth," I knew that I would have to focus my complete attention on the Witness work in 1975.

# Chapter 7

# *My Expulsion*

Jehovah's Witnesses practice a severe form of shunning, which is directed at members who are dis-fellowshipped (excommunicated) and those who officially disassociate themselves. This includes family members and even young ones.

## My Personal Experience

In my search to find employment, I finally landed a job pumping gas for the police at their headquarters. Although it was a part-time job, I was happy with getting a paycheck every week and buying the things necessary to change my poor image. I landed my second part-time job at Lee Simms Home Made Chocolates working as a porter.

One day while scrubbing chocolate off the floors, a familiar face walked in to make a purchase. She was a Jehovah's Witness from another congregation. Jehovah's Witnesses have different congregations such as the east, north, and south unit. I belonged to the east unit, she belonged to the west unit. Officially we had never met, but I had seen her before at one of the assemblies. She was not only a beautiful young lady, she was very kind and friendly.

After striking up a conversation with her, we exchanged phone numbers and a friendship ensued. Soon after, I developed feelings for her and fell in love. I kept the relationship secret from my parents because I was still under their microscope and they critiqued every move I made. That was short-lived because they soon found out through her mother. She had informed them of the courtship and brought to their attention that I was calling and visiting her home on a regular basis. She explained to them that she was concerned about our kissing and petting, as she had witnessed many times.

Once my parents revealed these things to me, they wanted to know why I didn't inform them of the courtship. I explained that I thought they would not approve of it. Soon, a meeting was arranged to discuss the nature of our friendship. We went to her parents' home and sat down with her parents and discussed the matter. Dad began quoting articles from various Jehovah's Witness literature focusing on the rules of dating, stating that we should not be dating if we weren't ready for marriage.

During the meeting, it seemed as if the focus was only on me. Dad wanted to know what my real motive was. Knowing what he was getting at I blurted out marriage, hoping to placate him. That did not impress him; he was implacable, saying that I wasn't ready for any type of relationship, let alone marriage. At the end of the meeting, both families disapproved of our courtship, saying we were too young and not established enough in life. Thus, we were barred from seeing each other ever again. I sat there stagnant, with all kinds of thoughts crossing my mind. I then realized that my life didn't belong to me, even when it came down to choosing someone to love.

That night as I laid in my bed I was crushed and felt hopeless, because I loved her; perhaps puppy love, but love nevertheless. After getting over my hurt, I carried on with my life and resumed with the Witness work.

It would be a year before I met someone I took interest in. We were introduced to one another by one of her in-laws who was a member of my congregation. Since she lived out of state, our courtship took place over the phone. During that time, she had made her parents aware of our friendship. I got a chance to speak with her father over the phone, asking his permission to visit her. Like my father, he was also an elder and very strict. He wanted to speak with my father before deciding. Once doing so, they both approved of the courtship, but under the condition that it had to be chaperoned. I took the trip with her in-law who had previously scheduled a visit.

Once arriving, I was introduced to her parents, who seemed to approve of me, which made me feel much more relaxed. I made sure I went wearing my best attire; my tight Jehovah's

Witness suit (only had one) and my best cologne. My new friend and I ventured out for a walk in the park and later that evening we dined out, then took in a movie. Her in-law kept a close eye on everything we did; even sitting directly behind us at the movie.

Later that evening, I awakened to use the bathroom but didn't know its location so I searched for it in the dark. What I thought to be the restroom, to my surprise, turned out to be her bedroom; she was sound asleep. Immediately leaving, I was grabbed by the arm by her father (who came out of nowhere) asking me, where are you going? After explaining that I thought it was the bathroom, the look on his face suggested that I was lying. He directed me towards the bathroom and waited outside until I was done. I was at a complete loss for words because I knew what he was thinking, especially finding me entering her bedroom in my underwear.

The next morning, he revealed to his in-law what he had witnessed and she was not a bit happy about it. From then on he kept his eye on every move I made until my departure. While heading out, I tried to explain to the in-law that the whole thing was a mistake and that I had no idea it was her bedroom. She just stared at me and said nothing.

I wasn't surprised that he had called my father because as soon as I returned home, Dad didn't waste any time questioning me about the incident. I didn't waver, and stuck with my story about mistaking her room for the bathroom. Whatever I said didn't matter because I was banished from ever seeing her again. For the second time in my life, a possible relationship was squashed.

After this episode, I felt it was time for me to be on my own, but I was not ready financially. I needed to find a better job, which would enable me to move away from the stress and duress of the day-to-day activity in our home that was being directed towards me.

Searching for better employment, I landed my first full-time job in New York City working as a porter for a small printing company called Proper Press. I now had the opportunity to save money and start looking for an apartment. In the meantime, I continued with my Witness work and became a part-time volunteer. I believed that Jehovah had blessed me with my new job and I wanted to prove my loyalty to him.

That's when another problem arose. My hormones had awakened and were twerking at full speed; twerking to the point that forced me to resume masturbating. I prayed for help and when that didn't work, I wrestled with the problem on my own and failed. My hormonal rush was like an itch that wouldn't go away. In short, I had tried to live a sinless life but there I was, again pleasuring myself. It got to the point that I considered approaching the elders about the problem, but was too embarrassed to follow through.

I believed the solution to my problem was to find a wife. I thought the search was going to be easy, but it wasn't. I went from congregation to congregation in search of Miss Wonderful but they weren't interested in dating me, perhaps because I was poor and sort of ragged-looking. I wasn't a bad-looking dude, just somewhat on the skinny side; perhaps from lack of proper nutrition.

Then again, the rules were very strict as far as finding a wife in the Jehovah's Witness circle. For example, in the Jehovah's Witness organization, you cannot focus your attention on multiple women. Doing so would be deemed unspiritual. The rules state that when contemplating a relationship, marriage should be your one and only goal. My mind-set said differently; women have different things to offer, and it's always a good idea to never put all your eggs in one basket. Although young, at least I knew that. That's why I felt that I had to give myself as many choices as possible, even if it was just being friends. But as mentioned, none seemed interested in me.

As I continued in my endeavor to find the right one, I realized that I was wasting my time. Trying to date a Jehovah's Witness woman was like dating a mannequin; in fact, a mannequin might even be better.

One autumn day in 1972, my brother returned to town for a short visit. He had recently been married and moved to upstate New York. I was happy to see him, and asked for his help in finding someone. That day was my lucky day. He mentioned that his wife's sister Carman was single and good-looking, with a nice body, but she wasn't a Jehovah's Witness. Jehovah's Witness or not, I wanted to meet her. Perhaps after getting to know her, I could sway her with my charm to take interest or perhaps join the organization.

I spoke with her over the phone and she sounded sweet and charming, as my brother stated; that's when I set up a weekend visit. But first, I had to get permission from my parents. After asking my father if it was ok to travel upstate with my brother and spend a few days with him and his family, he agreed. I believe he trusted me since I was baptized, although I was still under his microscope. I made sure not to mention the true nature as to why I wanted to travel. Knowing his track record, I would not have been given the permission.

In doing so, I realized that the road to paradise was not an easy one to follow; I was not the picture-perfect Jehovah's Witness I tried to pretend I was. It would soon be revealed and in the end, I would pay a heavy price for my imperfections.

During my travel, it was the first time I got to see the countryside and it was spacious and beautiful. We were traveling at the most beautiful and colorful season of the year. The autumn leaves displayed a rainbow of vibrant red and orange leaves that brought joy and calm to my soul. I never felt more relaxed in my life.

My brother and I conversed about the girl I was getting ready to meet and he offered up more details about her; one of which was very alarming. During our conversation, he mentioned that she had a medical problem, and before I could ask what it was, he interjected and asked me a fatuous question. He wanted to know if I would be interested in a girl who was crippled or in a wheelchair. What type of question is that? I asked. How crippled is she? He started laughing at my questions, and that's when I thought he was just kidding around. He reassured me that she was a fine sister and that I had nothing to worry about.

We pulled into the station and caught a taxi to his mother-in-law's house, where he was temporarily staying with his wife and new child. I was introduced to everyone and there she stood, the finest lady I had seen in a long time, which startled me. My brother was certainly right about her looks; but there was something else he didn't mention about her. This lovely woman was at least six months pregnant. If this is what he meant about her being crippled, he was certainly out of his mind. How does one equate being crippled with being pregnant?

Suddenly she made her move towards me and sent signals through her body language; moving close, breathing heavy, and making direct eye contact. She had several salient features, including, primarily, her humongous, mountain-grown ass, which was bursting through her tight jeans. My brother's wife had similar features. Perhaps that's why he fell for her hook, line, and sinker; he was mesmerized by her ass. They should have been named the butt sisters.

In all my days, I had never seen an ass that big and it startled me. Not even the women in my girly magazines displayed asses that big. It startled me to the point that I felt a bulge in my pants. My Jehovah's Witness brain told me not to look but she left me no choice and I couldn't resist the temptation. As I tried not to stumble over myself, unconsciously, my eyes were glued. She also had voluptuous breasts that were bursting through her cleavage and it was a sight for sore eyes. She was a little taller than me and they fell in line with my face; I was flabbergasted. In the back of my mind I knew that Jehovah was watching me and was displeased by my reaction towards her.

Dumbstruck, there I stood, face-to-face with a sexy pregnant woman. She invited me to go along with her to the local market, where we conversed in private. She explained her pregnancy to me, saying that her boyfriend had abandoned her once finding out she was knocked up. I asked her why she didn't tell me she was pregnant when we talked over the phone. Her response was that she was afraid I wouldn't be interested in her.

48

As we walked, her hips were humming in the wind. It didn't take her long to express how she felt about me; she expressed love at first sight, and wanted me to be her man. I must admit that those words made me feel good; I wanted to be loved by someone. However, I had no intentions of being involved with someone in her condition.

On returning to her mother's house, I was in for another surprise. I wasn't made aware of the fact that she was the mother of two young girls. Now here they were, rushing to greet her. I was disappointed at my brother for not filling me in on all the details about her before making our trip. Although attractive, this was a girl I didn't see a future with.

Sleeping over that night, I was awakened by my new friend at about two in the morning. She was wearing a sexy, see-through, white gown with breasts fully exposed and no panties. She had come to kiss me goodnight, but wanted more than just a kiss. As she rolled her tongue around in my mouth I had no idea what she was doing. I had never French kissed before and it felt strange, but it also turned me on. I laid there in complete silence, letting her take complete control over me. She continued the tease to the point where I completely forgot that I was a Jehovah's Witness. The soft, little kisses she planted on my ear got my blood boiling hot. I was completely hard now and there was no hiding it. Then she made her move.

As she mounted me, I suddenly started coming back to my senses and reminded her that I was a Jehovah's Witness and what we were doing was wrong. Countless times I asked her to stop but she ignored my pleas. As she reached down and guided me slowly inside of her, I didn't know what to expect, being a virgin. I must admit that whatever she was doing felt good, but feeling guilty about what was taking place bothered me. But then it was too late. I was already inside of her. The guilt went away as she started making small talk, whispering and licking on my ear as she worked me. She pressed hard against me, rocking in a quick fashion; her mouth by my ear moaning softly I love you drove me nuts, and was just too much for me to handle.

Suddenly, my body felt like a coffeepot ready to percolate. In no time I felt a strong, wonderful sensation, which started in my toes and worked its way up to my head. My body began to shake. With her hands covering my mouth, I groaned in ecstasy. It was one of the best feelings I ever had; 100 percent better than the payoff of masturbation. It was short and very intense; say approximately two minutes. I felt relieved, but also perplexed.

After cleaning me with a wet towel, she found my lips again and gave me a very passionate, lust-filled kiss and made her way to her room. As I laid there like the mannequin I was, staring up at the ceiling with thoughts racing through my mind, guilt set in again. There was no need to feel perplexed; I was a traitor to Jehovah, and it didn't take me long to realize that I showed no self-control whatsoever. I couldn't believe that I had just committed fornication. During my youth, I had been taught that I would be killed by God if I ever committed the act.

The next morning, on my way back home, I sat back in my train seat full of thought. I knew if I revealed my sin I might be punished by the elders, but didn't know to what extent. I knew that any follower who strayed beyond the *Watchtower*'s rigid boundaries was subject to that. I certainly didn't tell my brother out of fear he would spill the beans to our parents, yet I had to decide if I was going to confess my sin.

Once home I continued attending the Kingdom Hall meetings and went out in the field service almost every week as though nothing ever happened. But my sin laid heavy on my mind constantly, to the point that I couldn't think straight. It kept reminding me of my wrongdoing. Also, I felt the wrath of Jehovah following me around like a plague. There was never a day that didn't pass that I knew He would punish me, and kept thinking something bad was going to happen.

Up until that point I had gotten away with it but enough was enough; I couldn't take the pressure of feeling guilty, and had to reveal my sin. I soon set up a meeting with the elders of the Kingdom Hall I attended. They were assigned to the judicial committee and would judge me that day. I was taken into the conference room, where we discussed my wrongdoing. I told them my story and was contrite about my mistake.

As I revealed my sin, some seemed to enjoy my story, especially as I got into the sexual details of it; they were drooling, really! I remember the questions being asked. So, you planned to have sex? Were the lights off? Did you use a condom? How many times did you do it?

As the questioning continued, I was asked why I hadn't pushed her off me. I explained that I couldn't because she was pregnant, and I didn't want to hurt the baby. The baby? What baby? they asked. I explained that she was pregnant. They just stared at me in disbelief; now I was sure to be condemned.

After giving all the details, I was asked to step outside the conference room and wait while they made their decision. While doing so, I became frightened at the thought that mercy was the last thing on the minds of those who judged me.

Then the verdict came in. They deemed me an unrepentant wrongdoer who'd had sex with a married, pregnant woman. I disagreed and explained that she was not married. Interjecting, they said it didn't matter; I had sinned against Jehovah and had to be dis-fellowshipped from the congregation. I tried to convince them that I was repentant but they threw me out anyway. The instructions given were that I could continue to attend meetings at the Kingdom Hall but I had to sit in the back row. My expulsion was to be announced to the congregation at their convenience.

Now I was afraid they would pass the information off to my parents before I returned home, and I honestly wasn't sure if I would be living on the street that night. There was no way Dad was going to let me stay at home, and I was too shameful to face him. Knowing this I contacted my brother who had been previously thrown out, as mentioned earlier. After explaining my ordeal, he agreed to give me housing on a temporary basis if I were to be thrown out.

Returning home, I headed straight to my room, avoiding my parents at all cost. I even skipped dinner that night out of fear of facing them. But to my surprise, the judicial committee never contacted them. To me it was a big relief. But in the back of my mind, I knew my sin would be revealed more sooner than later.

The following week, I attended the Friday Kingdom Hall meeting. This would be the meeting where they would announce my expulsion. At the end of services, the elder who had taken the lead in the conference room approached the podium. As words spilled out of his mouth into the mic I was overwhelmed with embarrassment and headed for the exit. Before exiting, I could hear the announcement:

"We have an announcement to make; to keep God's organization clean, we have decided on dis-fellowshipping Brother Randy Thomas for conduct unbecoming a Christian."

Fearing the worst, and feeling abashed, I headed out to my brother's apartment; I didn't wait for my parents to evict me. It would have devastated me even further.

I soon came to the realization that baptism as a Jehovah's Witness is a binding verbal contract with the *Watchtower* society. What it meant was that unless I repented of my perceived sins in an acceptable way before a tribunal of church elders, I would forevermore be subjected to a life of shunning and ostracism by all church friends and family.

Then it happened; Jehovah's Witnesses I had known all my life now refused to make eye contact with me or speak to me. Anything I had ever known that had given me comfort or security was ripped from under me. The wheels had fallen off; everything was gone. My relationship with my parents and siblings hit the skids; they completely cut me off, avoiding me like the plague. They made it clear that they were having nothing to do with me. I was to be shunned without an acknowledgement of my existence; devoid of human courtesy and compassion. I might as well have been living on the moon because I suddenly found myself alone.

Out of guilt, I continued going to the Kingdom Hall meetings, sitting in the rear as instructed with my tongue clinging to the roof of my mouth. Members would stare at me but would never come near me; perhaps fearing a demon would jump off onto them. To them I was considered an apostate and viewed by all with fear.

At times, Dad would whisper in my ear and encourage me to repent, saying that the devil was out to stumble and confuse me. Other than that, he didn't have much more to say. What he said stayed in my mind daily, and I doubted everything I did, every move I made. I still wanted a relationship with my family, and felt that since I was no longer under the protection of Jehovah, I would still need them if anything happened to me while I was out in the "bad" world.

Going to the Kingdom Hall was the only time I could see Mom. I hoped that she would come to my rescue, but she didn't bat an eye towards me. I came forth from her own body; she nursed me, and cared for me through illness. Now a young adult, I'm suddenly rejected by her simply because she sought to be true to her conscience and to Jehovah. Some mothers even defend their children after they've committed grievous crimes. Here, I had never done anything except commit fornication, and she acted as if I was a horrible person, a grave disappointment, which I guess she needed to believe to justify her behavior toward me.

I felt that after all the things I went through with her as a child, I never thought she would turn her back on me. To her, blood ties meant nothing anymore. From now on the only contact with me would be when only necessary! I was completely banished from her love and sympathy.

After giving the thought some matter, at that time, I kind of agreed with the way she treated me. The *Watchtower* society instructed their members not to give in to blood ties when it comes down to a dis-fellowshipped loved one. The July 15, 1963, *Watchtower* (p. 443) goes into this rule in detail. Under the title, "Family Responsibility in keeping Jehovah's Worship Pure," they refer to the relative not living in the home:

> What if a person cut off from God's congregation unexpectedly visits dedicated relatives? What should the Christian do then? If this is the first occurrence of such visit, the dedicated Christian can, if his conscience

53

permits, carry on family courtesies on that particular occasion. However, if his conscience does not permit, he is under no obligation to do so. If courtesies are extended, though, the Christian should make it clear that this will not be made a regular practice…The excommunicated relative should be made to realize that his visits are not now welcomed as they were previously when he was walking correctly with Jehovah.

Taking this to heart, I followed the same routine every day of going to work and going to the meetings. I still felt that I was a Jehovah's Witness and wanted to be loved by my family and friends. Besides, the weeks of shunning took a terrible toll on me and I needed to change that. I could either go back to the Kingdom Hall and be reinstated or continue to live the lonely life I was living. After pondering the situation, I suddenly realized that in my entire life, people had always been telling me what to do and how to think, only for what they wanted. Now I had my freedom and started thinking twice about giving it up just to please others. Although lonely, I enjoyed my new freedom, but it would come at a costly price.

# Chapter 8

# *Running Wild*

Now free, I wandered as a man with no direction, no friends, and no purpose, without any kind of studying and very little skills. My belief about myself determined most of my actions; low self-esteem, and most of the time after returning from work, I confined myself to my brother's apartment, for I had nowhere else to go. As the months passed by, I thought about finding my own apartment. I also sensed that my brother and his girlfriend were growing a little weary of me, perhaps because I was invading their privacy. I also knew that I had exhausted my visit, and it was time for me to move on and take control of my life.

Then, just like that, I was laid off from my job and filed for unemployment. The funds didn't pay enough for me to rent an apartment but enough to rent a room, which I was in search of.

Then the thought of Carmen came across my mind. We were still in contact with each other over the phone, and perhaps she could convince her mother to take me in. After arranging a visit, I gathered my belongings (which didn't amount to much) and was on my way.

After arriving, I explained my situation to her mother. She was shocked about the treatment I'd received from my family after being expelled from the organization. She promised to take the matter up with her husband later and was kind enough to let me stay over for a few days until a decision was made. Carmen was now eight months pregnant and just about ready to give birth. Viewing her body, I noticed that her breasts were twice the size they were the last time I had seen her and it was a complete turn-on. I had not had sex with anyone since being with her and the memories of that occasion ignited my fire.

Just as soon as her parents stepped out for church that Sunday morning, we began tearing at each other. Once again our tongues and lips were wrestling. Not once did I think about being a Jehovah's Witness as I had in our previous engagement with sex and enjoyed every minute of it.

All my emotions came out with this woman. She was the only friend I had in the world. The truth be told, once I got another taste of sex, I couldn't go without it. I needed it morning, noon, and night. It was the antidote for all my problems at the time because it made me forget about anything negative. I had found something that made me happy, and happiness was the only thing I was in search of.

That afternoon, her mother gave me the bad news that I couldn't stay with them. Her excuse was that the little room that they had was being reserved for the new baby. This I accepted and was soon on my way. Before boarding my train, the thought of my brother and his new wife came across my mind. They had found their own apartment and lived in the same town. They were also Jehovah's Witnesses, and had to follow the rules pertaining to me being dis-fellowshipped; I couldn't ask to stay with them, so I forgot about the idea.

Back in New Jersey, I began looking for a rooming house but found no vacancies. In the meantime, I lived on the streets and made it the best way I knew how. Soon my unemployment check ran out and I filed for an extension. Once it was granted, I knew that I would have to look for work soon because the extension was very short. I also continued making frequent trips to see Carmen almost every other weekend. During that time, she gave birth to a baby boy. One thing I noticed during those visits was that she was at odds with her mother; always arguing. Soon she would move out of her mother's home and move in with her best girlfriend, minus her two children. The court gave her mother custody of them for one reason or the other.

During one of my visits, I explained to her my difficulty in finding a room, and she suggested that I come live with her. I jumped at the opportunity immediately and was happy to leave the state of New Jersey.

My first order of business was to find a job. I was successful, and found one in a chair factory. It didn't pay much, but I saved enough for us to rent a small apartment.

A few months passed, and we started going out for entertainment. Finding a babysitter was not that difficult; either her mother or best girlfriend would watch her child. We headed out to a bar that she was familiar with called The 218. I had never been in a bar before and can remember being very nervous.

After finding our seats, I observed people shooting pool, listening to a live band, dancing on a small dance floor, and sitting around the bar, being served drinks by a pretty barmaid. I had never seen a barmaid before and she was most certainly eye candy. Her exotic style of dress caught my eye. With her moon eyes, she stared at me long and hard and in a peculiar way, which aroused my passion. Carmen didn't seem to notice the exchange between us because she was too busy chatting with her girlfriends.

Before the night ended, she invited me out onto the dance floor. There was only one problem; I wasn't a good dancer. While living at home I didn't have much practice, yet I tried to do my best. As we danced, I could feel the barmaid's eyes burning a hole in the back of my skull. There was no doubt that we were attracted to one another. I think she had it in for me ever since laying eyes on me and because I was the new kid on the block.

For the first time in my life I felt real freedom, and wanted to get out more. At times, Carmen trusted me and let me venture out alone, which turned out to be a big mistake. With that type of freedom I began bar hopping, and that's when all my problems began. I started running wild, and I engaged in drinking, swearing, and women. It was like coming out of a cave after spending twenty years inside and seeing the whole world spread before me. I felt unshackled, and couldn't have been more excited. I was finally out from under my parents' umbrella of protection and authority and was free to do, or not do, whatever I wanted. I purposely made myself a target for other women to enjoy and engaged in this behavior shamelessly.

For example, while out one night at The 218, I ran into my favorite barmaid, who was working that night. Seeing me out alone, she asked that I wait for her until she got off work. While escorting her home, she explained that she lived with her parents and they would not like the idea of her having company at this late hour. She then led me to the nearby woods, and that's when the fireworks began. We began kissing and tearing passionately at each other, and shortly thereafter, had sex on the hard ground. During our engagement, she passionately sucked on my neck, which turned on my fire even more. Then it started to drizzle lightly but I didn't give two shits; who the hell cares about rain in the heat of passion? We continued tearing at each other but had to stop because it started to rain even harder. I most certainly didn't want to create a muddy mess. I wasn't going home in this condition without arousing suspicion.

After escorting her home, I hurried my way back to my apartment and was happy to find Carmen asleep. After taking a shower, I quietly slid into bed without waking her. While that worked out, there were fireworks the next morning.

While arguing about me being out so late, she noticed the hickey marks on my neck, even though I was completely oblivious to it, and demanded an explanation. It was a scary moment because she was in a fit of rage, and rightfully so. Knowing that I was busted, I was contrite with her, saying that I was out slow dancing with someone when she started sucking on my neck, but never admitted to having sex with that person. She fell for the bogus excuse hook, line, and sinker. I had gotten away with it this time, but now I had to be more careful with my whore-mongering.

From there on in, I sneakily started having sex with women who were only interested in just that. I became an unconscionable profligate young man when it came down to doing so. I didn't mind being a new piece of meat in town. My hormones were pulling in all different directions and I didn't know how to control them and didn't care. I also knew that Carmen was very suspicious of me, and I gave her reason to be. We were at each other's throats constantly because of my bad behavior. That's when I decided to stop my whore-mongering and spend more time at home. She made me promise to control my horny instincts, which I did. The months that followed were very pleasant and I fell in love with her.

As time moved on, I lost my job in the factory but found another one, although part-time. I took the job as an "apple knocker" on an apple and strawberry farm. Being unskilled, that was the only work I could get at that time. It was a low-paying job with no job security. Most farm workers are paid based on how many buckets or bags they pick of whatever crop they harvest. This is known as the "piece rate." Payment in this format has some drawbacks. First, if workers are being paid by how much they pick, this acts as a disincentive to take breaks for water, food, or shade. I took so many it cut into my productivity and thus cut into my pay. At the end of the day, my being paid by piece rate amounted to less than the minimum wage.

Not being able to pay rent, and always short on money, Carmen and I were always engaged in argument. She also had a problem with me not being able to find a decent job. Soon we were evicted and she moved back in with her parents. I was not allowed that luxury, which left me homeless. I was angered that her parents wouldn't take me in, even knowing that I had no place else to go. My relationship with Carmen went straight downhill after that and once again I started whore-mongering, which included trying to find someone to take me in.

After so many empty romances and job disappointments, I decided to move on to another area in upstate New York. All my adventures brought the same results; nothing. As the saying goes, "Nothing from nothing leaves nothing." I couldn't name one thing that I had accomplished other than getting laid.

## Chapter 8: Running Wild

Looking back, my behavior towards Carmen changed as soon as she gave birth. She was preoccupied with taking care of her newborn, which gave me time to run wild. I realized that I had wasted so much time displaying my foolish tendencies at the expense of others, and now it was time to move on.

# Chapter 9

## *Super Fly*

My wanderings brought me back to Jersey City, New Jersey, searching for I knew not what. I had no idea what I would do or how I would support myself while on this new journey.

My first order of business was to find a job; something I accomplished immediately. It was in a clothing factory and paid the minimum wage. All in all, it paid enough money for me to rent a furnished room, which didn't cost much in those days.

Since being away from home, I hadn't seen or heard from anyone else in the family other than my brother upstate. I contemplated on visiting my parents, but dropped the idea; they would have nothing to do with me. Besides, I would run into them sooner or later, it was just a matter of time; and then it happened.

One morning while on my way to work, I came across my mother and some of her Jehovah's Witness friends standing on the street corner peddling the *Watchtower* message. I purposely crossed her path with the hope for eye contact and perhaps engagement. Noticing me she stood there, saying nothing. This saddened me, of course, but I continued on my way.

Once stable with a job, it was time to find some new friends and a lover; someone to fill the void.

I sat for hours ordering drinks at bars, waiting for a stray to cross my path. Then it happened. At the other end of the bar was a lovely, dark-skinned lady dressed in a black, with voluptuous breasts, wearing red lipstick and had long black hair. She was staring directly at me and didn't bat an eye. She reminded me of the lovely barmaid I had met in upstate New York. As she continued to stare and flirt with her eyes, I made my move.

First, I asked the bartender to send her a drink. After accepting it, she sent me one in return. I thought about approaching her and introducing myself, but vacillated out of fear of her having a boyfriend lurking around somewhere; I had to be careful. For the next half-hour I watched her, and believed her to be alone.

After exchanging a few more drinks, I got up the courage and approached her. After introducing myself, we engaged in conversation for the next hour. Upon doing so, I noticed that she most certainly exaggerated certain characteristics, such as the lipstick and makeup she wore; it was way too much. During our conversation, she stated that she had met me someplace before but couldn't remember. Of course, I lied and said that she did look familiar, and suggested that we had met sometime the previous year. With me, I would say anything just to get laid.

As the conversation continued, she wanted to know if I lived alone and if I would like any company. This was my lucky day, and after purchasing some beer and pickled pig feet, we were on our way. After leaving the bar, I noticed her style of dress and her features more clearly. Inside the bar, it was dark so I couldn't get a clear picture. Now she was in full view. She wore seven-inch heels, a skintight black silk dress and wore a black wig. To me, she resembled a prostitute, but that didn't bother me. I was only interested in getting laid.

Upon arriving at my place we downed the pickled pig feet and beer, then things began to get hot. As we French kissed, I most certainly noticed that her style of kissing was different from what I had experienced with others. However, I paid it no attention. After stripping and jumping into bed, we were engaged in foreplay when I noticed a few strange things. First, I started taking her bra off but she refused. I told her there was no need to be shy and upon removing it, I was shocked to find her bra stuffed with toilet tissue. Her breasts were extremely tiny; golf ball size. The next revelation would set everything off. While rubbing my fingers between her legs, they came across a small object. Right away I knew what it was and realized that I was in bed with a man; a drag queen, and all hell broke loose.

After kicking him to the floor, I turned on the lights, and there I stood face-to-face with a naked, ugly man; it was disgusting. After snatching off his wig I began roughing him up and dragged him out into the hallway. After kicking him down the stairs I returned to my room and collected his clothes and wig and tossed them to him while screaming obscenities at him. The realization that I had been kissing and in bed with a man made me feel unclean. I commenced taking a shower and gargled almost a whole bottle of Listerine until my mouth was raw. I then asked myself, how could I not know that it was a man? The truth of the matter was that I knew very little of the world I lived in. I had no life skills and had a lot to learn, and in a hurry.

During that time, I had a poor wardrobe and needed to change it to look hip. Most black men during that era bought their clothing from a flea market place located on Canal Street in New York City. Looking sharp was fine, but I only had a jingle in my pockets, so I couldn't buy much.

While hanging out in bars to fill the void of loneliness, I ran into an old classmate who was a musician and played a mean bass guitar. He helped me bring more spice into my life by introducing me to a different type of nightlife other than the sleazy bars I was hanging out in. He had landed a gig in Harlem at a place called the Blue Book, a jazz club, located on 145th and St. Nicolas Avenue. He invited me to go along with him and it turned out to be my official introduction to the nightlife in New York City. The music was pumping, the whisky flowed, and fine ladies packed the dance floor. It was one of the best times of my young, misguided life.

In upstate New York and Jersey City I had gotten used to bars, pool tables, low-class people. But Harlem had a much different setting. It was more cosmopolitan, full of adventure and had a wonderful nightlife. From 125th Street all the way up to 155th were classy clubs. I even met celebrities; Harry Bellefonte, actress Sheila Frasier, and Barbara O, just to name a few.

As I continued visiting various clubs I got so hooked on Harlem, I decided to give up my rented room and relocate there. I found a rooming house on 147th Street and St. Nichols Avenue, right in the heart of the club district and moved in shortly. During weekends, I visited various clubs and I made friends with many people. I also met a young lady I was attracted to who could perhaps end my whore-mongering. She lived in Queens, New York, and was special to me. The only problem was that I didn't own a car, or have a license to drive one even if I did, so we remained just friends.

During this period of my life, I was an impressionable young man. There were many (black exploitation) movies that were playing in Harlem, and two that caught my attention were named *Super Fly* and *Shaft*. I remember heading out to see the movie *Super Fly* clearly, because I never made it to the box office.

After taking the A train and getting off on 42nd Street, I was accosted by an older black man who claimed he was a sailor visiting town. He asked if I knew where a certain address was. At first I refused to help him, but then changed my mind. He seemed harmless, so I offered to help him. He was looking for a brothel off 42nd Street. Not being a street-smart person, I had never heard of a brothel before so I thought he meant hotel. I asked if he had an address, which he did.

While I was leading him to it, he stopped a stranger on the street and asked if he could assist us in finding the address, to which he agreed. The stranger, an older black man, led us to an address located in a back alley. It turned out to be the whorehouse he was looking for.

As I headed back to the box office, the so-called sailor asked if I could do him a favor. He wanted me to hold his wallet containing his credit cards and $200 dollars. He claimed that he was afraid of being ripped off while inside the brothel. He promised to give me $100 once he returned. I agreed. He took out his wallet, wrapped it in a large, white handkerchief, and before handing it over to me, he warned me not to run away with his money. The stranger interjected and suggested that I put my money and watch inside the same handkerchief, and unwittingly, I stepped into his trap by doing so. After wrapping tape around the handkerchief and handing it over to me, both men entered the whorehouse and like the idiot I was, I stood outside in the cold for almost half an hour waiting for him to return. When that

64

didn't happen, the thought of stealing the bundle crossed my mind. In just a blink of an eye I turned from Mr. Nice Guy to a thief. I didn't vacillate for one minute and nervously left in a hurry, just in case they reappeared.

After I flagged down a cab, I asked the driver to take me to Queens. I wanted to surprise my new friend and ask her out to the movies. I now had $300 extra dollars in my pocket and I was happy.

As we approached the Queens Borough bridge, I started un-wrapping the bundle. I was proud that I had screwed the sailor out of his dough; but to my surprise, there was nothing inside the handkerchief but shredded newspaper. How could that be? I thought. I watched him put everything in the handkerchief and wrap it in tape. I couldn't understand how he managed to fool me. Then the reality set in; I had gotten robbed while trying to rob the robber. Even while I was trying to be a thief it didn't work; it said a lot about who I was.

Now everything had changed. I asked the cab driver to take me back to 42nd Street, to track the men down. I had no money to pay him, but he demanded something. The only thing I had that was worth anything was my new super fly brim. He accepted it as collateral, and I went back looking for the men but to no avail, they were long gone.

After thinking about what had just transpired, I realized that the sailor was no sailor, and that the stranger was his accomplice. With no money to get home, I approached an officer at the station and told him my story. He was kind enough to let me board the train free of charge; also saying that I should be more aware of my surroundings in the Big Apple.

Once home, I sat and wondered why I was so gullible, and wondered why I wasn't smart enough to notice the scam. Anybody can spot a sucker, and they spotted me.

The following weekend, I headed out to see the movie *Super Fly* and once doing so, it changed my whole personality. I loved the movie so much that I viewed it many times for reinforcement. Now I was an indestructible young man and wanted to dress like the character in the movie, Ron O'Neal. I headed to the flea market and purchased an assortment of colored platform shoes, bell-bottom pants, a white imitation leather coat and a few colorful brims. Over time I grew an Afro and some serious sideburns with a well-groomed mustache. I also changed the way I walked and talked. I went from walking like a straight-up robot to a signified bopper. I no longer sounded like a Jehovah's Witness parrot and spent hours in the mirror practicing curse words like *motherfucker* and *shit*, until I got it right. To further emulate the characters in the movie, I turned to smoking cigarettes. In the black community, there were plenty of billboard signs featuring cigarette products. The only problem I had with that was, I didn't know how to inhale. Once I learned, I thought I was on my way to becoming a sophisticated young man.

On viewing myself in the mirror, I believed that this is what a black man was supposed to look like. I had now officially interjected myself into the world and knew that I was ready; for what, I did not know. I did know that I had to change my job situation in the money department if I wanted to keep in style. With that said, I landed a better-paying job at an insurance firm in downtown New York called AIG. My job duties included domestic and messenger work. Sooner or later I would move into another rooming house on 153rd Street, where I continued with my irresponsible behavior of bar hopping and chasing women.

On 148th Street there was a bar called the Starr Lounge, and it would be my best hanging out spot. It was the best place if you wanted to find a quick lay. Plus, it was walking distance from where I lived.

One night while I was out searching for a stray, I met a lady 10 years my junior named Serena. She lived in the rough section of the Bronx in New York City and was an egocentric, demanding person. This wasn't going to be an easy lay. Since everything revolved around her, I became a yes-man and complied passively with whatever she said. I thrived on the adulation of my new friend.

During our friendship, she constantly talked about sex and how good she was in bed, but offered me no sex. We were out one night and for more than an hour, she belabored her point about the importance of having a good sex partner. I remember her asking me a question; a question that I mistook. She wanted to know if I got down. I responded, you'd better believe it, which brought a smile to her face. The question she asked I thought involved dancing; but was to find out later that it didn't.

After taking in a weekend movie, I invited her to my room and the fireworks began. During the most exciting foreplay, she asked me to lick her. I began licking her arms, breasts, and stomach. Her fingers were glued to my Afro, urging me on and encouraging my movement. As I could feel the little shivers of pleasure shooting through her, I was sure that I had hit the spot. As I dragged my tongue across her voluptuous breast, she asked what I was waiting for and reminded me that I said I went down. I hadn't the faintest idea of what she was talking about when suddenly she grabbed my Afro and pulled my head down between her legs. After wrapping them around my neck, she started rubbed my face into her vagina repeatedly. I could feel the acrid sting of her pubic hair in my nostrils and the smell of fish. It was harsh and unpleasant. Trying to break free and hold my breath at the same time seemed to be a mission impossible. Finally, I managed to wrestle her out of bed onto the floor. Now she was angry and went into a rage. She cursed me and stormed out the door.

The next day, I called and apologized for ruining the night. I felt abashed by my inability to satisfy her. She reminded me that it was me who said that I went down. That's when I realized what she meant, and simply explained that I thought she was talking about dancing and getting down on the dance floor. I also explained that I had never participated in oral sex before and that I wasn't quick with catch phrases. As I explained more of my background, she understood me a little better and absolved me.

As our friendship continued, she convinced me to give up my room and move in with her. She lived in a beautiful two-bedroom apartment that made my room look like a shoe box. Now it was sex every night, where she focused more on oral sex than anything else. I always asked myself, why does it smell like fish? How long can I hold my breath while doing this? Many nights I pretended to be either sleep or sick so I could get out of doing it every night. However, that backfired because we had many confrontations on the subject matter of me refusing to perform every night and as a result, our relationship soured. It would also set the course for the rest of my life.

After returning from work one day, I couldn't enter the apartment. She had deliberately changed the lock. Speaking through the door, she said I needed to find another place to live. I asked her to give me a chance to find a room but she was adamant, saying that I should come back the next day and pick up my belongings, which didn't amount to much.

Once doing so, she placed them in two large garbage bags. I wound up getting rid of what I didn't need, to make the load lighter. Since it was winter, I kept the things that would keep me warm. Now, I didn't have much; a match box couldn't carry my property.

At the time of my eviction, I didn't have enough money to rent a room. And even if I did, none were available in that area, including my old room; it had been rented out. I also didn't have friends in Harlem who would take me in. Perhaps I could have gone to a homeless shelter, but at that time in my life, I didn't know about those services.

After being on the street for a week, the thought of an old friend came to mind. Not having his phone number, I boarded the train and headed to Jersey City in search of him. He had lived in the same rooming house I had previously lived in before leaving Jersey. Perhaps he would let me bunk with him until I gathered enough money to rent a place of my own.

Once arriving, I was shocked to see that the rooming house had been demolished due to a fire. My next move was to call my parents' home, but quickly forgot about the idea since they had always been oblivious to my welfare in the past. I had been told by them from the start that I could never speak to them until I returned to Jehovah and his Faithful Slave Class. I wasn't considered a loving child anymore. I was considered a child of Satan; an abomination before God.

In my last hope to find shelter I headed over to my brother's house, only to find that he had moved to an undisclosed location. Then the reality sank in that the process of dis-fellowshipping had quite literally cut me off from my family. Now I began walking around like one of the zombies from the *Walking Dead* with nowhere to go. As darkness fell and it began to get colder, I began to panic; my hands were freezing, and I needed to find a warm place and fast. That's when I found an apartment building and made it my home until I could do better. I headed to the rooftop landing that provided a small sleeping space where I couldn't be seen. It was completely isolated. Now I had a warm place to rest my body and lay my head. Since I didn't have a sleeping bag, I found some cardboard to sleep on. It was much better than sleeping on the marble surface. Living on a rooftop landing wasn't easy, of course. I had to find a way not to draw the attention of the tenants, landlord, or the police. I also had to get rid of my bright super fly coat and replace it with another. It most certainly brought attention to myself.

Whenever I left the building, I would leave nothing behind. It would be a dead giveaway that someone was loitering. During the day, I worked, but when I was off on the weekends, I spent most of my time visiting shopping malls and hospital waiting rooms, where it was warm. I also took the opportunity to use the facilities' rest rooms to clean and groom myself. It was harder to keep busy at night. I also had to make sure that I returned to the apartment building before it got too late. It would be harder getting buzzed in after eight in the evening.

After staying out of harm's way for a few weeks and working some overtime, I managed to save enough money to rent a room for a couple of weeks. Then I got the surprise of my life. Headed back to work the next day, I received a pink slip from my employer, informing me that I had been fired; my job performance was not acceptable. This was the saddest day of my life. I needed this job to sustain myself and reverse my homelessness.

Returning to the apartment complex that evening, I sat at the top of the stairs and was in thought, trying to figure out what to do next. What else could go wrong? I thought. How was I going to survive with no job? I was also worried about running out of money before I received unemployment compensation. I had to wait for four weeks before I could file for it because I was due another check from my former employer. To me, that seemed to be an eternity. It wouldn't be much, and I would exhaust those funds in a few days. It would be two weeks before I could file.

While waiting, I was barely getting enough food to eat or the necessities. I wasn't sure how long I was going to survive. My diet at that time consisted of canned foods, eating cold soup right out of the can, beef jerky, potato chips, dried fruit, and corn chips; hardly enough to fill a hungry stomach. I remember one night being so hungry I used trickery to satisfy my hunger pangs.

One evening while up on the roof, I noticed a pizza delivery van in front of the building. Once obtaining the number, I went to a nearby phone booth, called, and ordered a large pizza with everything on it. I remember trying to disguise my voice as if I were an affluent white man. The building's occupants were all white so I had to sound convincing.

Once the pizza man arrived, I met him at the front door and he handed me the pizza. Without paying him I slammed the door shut and headed straight to the roof and had a feast. I didn't care if he called the police or not, I only wanted to satisfy my hunger. I thought he would call the police but after watching him pull off, I put away those fears.

Now having much more time, I couldn't continue dodging in and out of the apartment building because I would certainly attract the attention of someone; and then it happened. Late one evening I was spotted loitering by one of the building's residents while heading to my usual spot. She immediately called the landlord, who lived on the first floor. They nabbed me, and I was questioned and held until the police arrived. The police wanted to arrest me for trespassing until I explained that I was homeless

and had nowhere else to go. It didn't matter to them; I was physically thrown out into the cold and threatened with arrest if I returned.

Now the cold and sadness sank in. I found myself out on the street, without having a plan of where to go or what to do. Then the thought of my best friend came to mind, wondering if he went through the same thing before committing suicide. He had been homeless after being kicked out by his Jehovah's Witness parents. Contemplating the same course of action raced through my mind. I was in the darkest part of my life, and wondered if it was still worth living. Those I would view as friends and contacts were completely gone and there was no one to take their place. With my hopes and dreams destroyed, my sexual escapades coming to a screeching halt, no resources or money, and no place to turn, what else was I to do? I thought.

The guilt, loneliness, abandonment, persecution, and ridicule from people I loved with all my heart was too much to bear. Those who once loved me, with one announcement that I was dis-fellowshipped, turned that love off in an instant. I had received the kiss of death. I know it sounds crazy, but the very foundation of my life was torn to pieces, and the shunning had been torturous to my soul; and it certainly had made suicide an option at that time in my life.

Being discombobulated, I also just didn't have the answers that I needed at that time when I was young and lost. I was tired, hungry, exhausted, cold, and I didn't have the energy to fight the battle anymore. I had been left adrift upon a stormy ocean, with no anchor to weigh me down, and no safe harbor in which to port; enough was enough. After giving it further thought, I did not want to give in to my exhaustion and forgot about the idea. It was time to move on before freezing to death.

To get out of the cold, I boarded the train in Jersey City and headed back to New York. I then boarded the A train. That would be my new home until I picked up my unemployment check. While managing to survive, I used those funds to rent a furnished room in Jersey City. The rent was sixty dollars per week. After moving in I breathed a sigh of relief; I was finally off the streets.

Knowing that unemployment compensation didn't last very long, I immediately started my search for work. Perhaps finding a good job would help me break out of this continued cycle of irresponsibility. I was lucky, and landed another factory job. After three months I had polished up my wardrobe, gained back the weight I had lost, and made a new friend. I started hanging out, and went right back to my old ways.

The year was 1976, and I continued to drink, party, and chase skirts. In a blink of an eye, I went from super fly to super fool.

Fueled by guilt, I had arrived at the truth that I was living a wicked life. From time to time I contemplated going back to the Kingdom Hall and being reinstated as a Jehovah's Witness. In these terms, I sought a resolution of the issues dominating my life. Then I got the surprise of my life; Jehovah's Witnesses were knocking on my door every other weekend trying to convince me to return. They knew my background and knew my entire family. They kept reminding me of Armageddon. Even though it didn't come in 1975, they advised me that it was coming soon, and I needed to change my direction.

That's when the thought entered my mind that perhaps they may be right; maybe 1975 was just a test. I believed this was at least in part, because in the past I had formed a deeply rooted layer in my mind about it and it was still an unchanging foundation, even though I was excommunicated.

In the back of my mind, I also continued to think that part of my problems in life stemmed from not being in the truth any longer and I was being punished by Jehovah. I had been warned in the past that bad things would come my way if I didn't return, and I believed after all that I went through, they were right.

From there on in, I started preparing myself mentally to go back to the Kingdom Hall and seek reinstatement as a Jehovah's Witness. Then, just like that, I put everything on hold and started questioning myself about reconsidering my decision; especially by an organization that had shown no compassion to me in the past and would doubtfully do so in the future if I were to commit another sin. All these years they had made me feel like I was worth nothing. To me, being excommunicated from a religious organization was one of the vilest practices possible. It was like having to go through a mass living bereavement daily.

But even after all the religion had put me through, deep down, I wanted to go back. Perhaps it had to do with my emotional dependence and it needed to be validated. Eventually, I would remain firm in my decision to rededicate myself to Jehovah. But first I had a few demons I needed to exorcise. I would have to endure a lot more before I reached my goal of reinstatement.

# Chapter 10

# *Boomerang*

As I struggled with my decision on changing my life for the better, I still had no vision; my vision went no further than my nose. Being uneducated and destitute, I resumed smoking and drinking, sometimes on an empty stomach, and was skinny as a train rail. For a while this led to the gradual stagnation of my soul. The level of education I had and the environment where I was raised were accurate indicators of my failure at most things I tried. During that time, I felt like there was always a Higher Power out there waiting to rip the rug out from underneath me no matter how hard I tried, and it was best to just not try at all because it didn't matter what I did, I was destined to fail. As Benjamin Mays said, "The tragedy in life doesn't lie in not reaching your goal. The tragedy lies in having no goals to reach."

Further trials and tribulations forced me to do a reality check. I didn't have confidence in myself and at times I suffered from anxiety, self-doubt, low self-esteem, poor self-worth, lack of direction, feelings of alienation, and difficulty adjusting to a "worldly" lifestyle. Sex was still my salvation, and I knew that if I continued my present course, it would lead to disaster.

Additionally, I didn't have the experience or knowledge of how the world works in general. I had nothing to contribute to progress and I knew it. I felt that I had wasted a lot of years chasing my tail, not knowing who I was or what my goal in life was. I believed that my life was something to be ashamed of. No matter what I put on, super fly clothes and all, I was an empty suit from the start. I was nothing but a clown, a clown in black face; one without a bank account, poor credit, and nothing to show for his life. What I failed to realize was that need is defined by the goal it aims at, and if limited, there's no goal, since there is no limit. It is said that if a man does not keep away from a source of infection, he will probably contract the disease. In such an instance, the outcome of my actions follows as a direct consequence of having neglected a rule of quarantine. The penalty I suffered for my violation was given because of my act.

In the past I had been warned, and because of my failure to learn, was convinced that the devil had been out to stumble and confuse me. While out in the world, I had spent several years without any desire for any type of relationship with God. But I was now convinced that the only way to gain his favor would be to return to the organization. I thought about the embarrassment of crawling back after so many years just to admit that I was a bad person. I felt that my decision to rejoin would have to be a sagacious one because without this move, worse things were likely to happen to me. Being cut off by people who were a huge part of my life one day and who ignored me like I no longer existed the next was a catastrophic life event that I had to deal with and I was happy it would end soon.

The truth of the matter was that I was raised from birth as one of the Jehovah's Witnesses, and knew of no other way of living. That's when I decided to take a new step toward a future, even as uncertain as it was to be. As mentioned, before returning, there were a few habits I needed to quit. The main one was smoking. As I tried to quit the habit, I did quit drinking and whore-mongering; although I was still horny.

Education-wise, I needed to better myself in that department. I applied and qualified for a government program called CETA, (Comprehensive Employment Training Act). CETA was an education program designed to train people to jumpstart their career in whatever their chosen field was. It also was a government-paid program that lasted six months. You were required to attend school five days a week, six hours a day, to get a government check every two weeks. Therefore, I had to quit my day job to make the requirements. With that in place, I was ready to make my move back to Jehovah.

As I started attending the weekly meeting at the Kingdom Hall, everyone seemed surprised. At first no one said anything to me and just gave me the evil eye. I was still considered a traitor by everyone. The more meetings I attended, the more smiles I received. My parents even spoke to me every now and then to encourage me even further. They responded to me in a manner that made me feel respected and cared about. They were showing me attention and I wanted it to last; forever!

From that time on, I missed very few meetings. My heart would soon be taken over by the Witnesses because of the attention I was being shown. Some of the members even sat in the vacant seats next to me. In the past, they wouldn't come near me, as though I had the plague or something worse.

It was also a thrill to see some of my siblings and former friends. I knew that I was well on my way back to becoming a Jehovah's Witness because I even participated in singing kingdom songs at the beginning and end of every meeting. I still knew the words by heart and sang out loudly. I even got a few looks, with smiles of approval, which made me sing even louder, like a trained parrot.

As time moved on I tried to contact my older brother to inform him of my latest actions and to seek his advice. I had developed in my mind the urgent need to be recognized and loved and was reaching out. He had gotten married and moved away to California. I wanted to let him know the good news that I was on my way back to righteous living and in March of 1977, wrote him this letter seeking his advice (taken out of my diary).

Greetings, Brother Larry! How are you in these hard times? Still putting forth that great effort in the faith? I wish I could say that I am, for I'm still in, around, and on, as you would say, the sinking ship of destruction. If you can spare a life jacket, or in other words, encouragement, send it to me first class. It would be nice to converse with you, for you are my brother.

Since being in the world, kinesthetic perception has developed to such a degree that my mind is uncomfortable. For it does not perform good motion, with a minimum of effort, to produce good and maximum results. Right now, I'm developing a secret

76

weapon, which will be a sure and valuable defensive tactic. This tactic is, of course, the word of God. Using this will enable me to ward off any wrongdoing and temptations.

Sidestepping is the next step. For when I see action, foolish action, coming my way, I would gain a more advantageous position by moving quickly out of range. Do you know that for at least a month I've been practicing this quick retreat? It's working because I've been turning down many unrighteous things.

I'm starting to attend meetings, and being the man I most likely should be. But there are a few things that are holding me back; smoking is one, and the need for sex is another.

I know I must try harder, and include prayer with this. Between me and you, for this line is personal, I haven't had sex in almost a month. It's good in some ways, but bad in another, because the feeling is much greater now than ever before, and controlling myself is like trying to control a sandstorm. You see, I only want one woman, not eight or nine, but one; one woman, who in time would want to live with me in marriage forever. I don't want to waste myself on the selfish women in the world. There must be a remedy.

Let me ask you a question please. If you knew a lady who had been associated with the truth, but not baptized, and stepped into the world like I did, would you try to speak words of encouragement to her, especially if she knew what I knew about the future of the world? Would you try to get her back on the right track, or just leave it alone?

She's a very lovely lady. She's got class and wit; the kind of lady who kills you with her smile and way of walking. I don't know everything about her, but as long as we are on the wrong road, both of us putting the pieces together might be one of the best things that could happen.

As you can see, I'm not selfish, but a loving person. In your return letter, advice is what I will be looking for. For it might be possible that I may be sidestepping the wrong way. Is your wife still as beautiful, kind, and considerate as when you first met her? Tell her to say a prayer for me, it might just help. Are your kids growing in the faith? Well good then, if they are. So, let me go, Larry, I have things to attend to. I hope that you and your beautiful family prosper.

Sincerely yours,
Love, Randy
P.S. I know when you received this letter you were surprised and had that old-time saying, "the face."

To further prove that I was sincere in my commitment to return to Jehovah, I wrote the following draft and a few letters to myself and entered them into my diary in the months of May through the month of December 1977. I would use it as proof that I had repented from my sins when facing the elders seeking reinstatement:

This month is a very strange month indeed. It is supposed to be May 10, 1977, and all is very cold and wet, like an ice age. But regardless of how the weather is, my standing with myself is getting to a degree that in the near future I will be able to smile, knowing that what I'm doing now, on this given day of May 11, 1977, ensures me of a good future. Clerical typing is my goal, and it consists of not just typing but spelling English, math, shorthand, bookkeeping, and operating a switchboard. Having these qualifications does ensure me of more than one job. My standing with my parents is becoming better, because I am attending my meetings.

Acquire Wisdom, taken from Proverbs 4:5-18:

Dear Randy, it is always good to acquire wisdom and understanding. Wisdom is the prime thing; it will exalt you, glorify you, if you embrace it. If we acquire this, the years of life will become many. The wicked one does not sleep unless they do badness, and their sleep had been snatched away, unless they cause a humble person to stumble. The wicked ones will feed themselves with the bread of wickedness, and the wind of violence. But the way of the wicked one is like the gloom.

As brothers and sisters, we should all safeguard our hearts, for out of it are the sources of life. We who have trouble with vulgar speech should remove from ourselves the crookedness of speech and the deviousness of lips we should put far away from us.

Those of us who are walking in integrity will walk in security, and we who are making our ways crooked will make him known in death. The days of the wicked ones will be cut short. It's simple because those who are looking for good, will keep seeking good things. And the ones searching for bad, it will come quickly upon him.

It is the lip of truth that will be firmly established forever, but the tongue of falsehood will be only as long as a moment.

Another way we can acquire wisdom is to watch who we walk with, because those who are walking with wise persons will become wise, but those who are having dealings with the stupid ones will fare badly.

One day soon I will be righteous because God is the one I love, but it must be proven. Wickedness gets no one anywhere. The righteous ones are eating to the satisfaction of their soul, but the belly of the wicked ones stays empty. And even in laughter, the heart is well in pain.

It's good to be wise, because the wise one fears God and is turning away from badness. But the stupid one is becoming devilish in his rotten ways. The fear of God is a good life, for it makes me turn away from the snare of death! Just imagine how beautiful life really is if we endeavor to serve the one and only God Almighty. The world will be just as beautiful and peaceful as it once was when the first two were created. For a few minutes in each one's life we seek enjoyment. It may be righteous, or unrighteous, but if it happens to be unrighteous, then we will lose out of enjoyment forever. You see, when we are doing wrong, the feeling with God isn't mutual.

After this letter, I continued attending meetings and prayed daily asking to be accepted back to full membership. After giving up the cigarettes, I met with the elders and asked for reinstatement. After going through a series of questions, I had to convince them that I had truly repented of my sin. After passing the entire question-and-answer test and showing them the above letters I had written, it was enough proof for them to reinstate me. I was placed on a probationary period of one year, which meant there were certain privileges in the congregation I would not be able to participate in. I was told that I could immediately go out in field service to preach, but not much more

After they announced my reinstatement, I was the new kid on the block. I will never forget that moment; everyone rushed to greet me with hugs and tears. The same people who didn't care whether I starved to death or not (fair weather friends) were now acting as though I was a complete partner.

# Chapter 11

## *Here Comes the Bride*

Since being away for so long, the first order of business was to be reprogrammed. I had to familiarize myself with the new and changed policies of the organization. I immediately started slipping back into inertia and started swallowing all the spiritual "food" again, as fast as the "faithful steward" could serve it. I got on the Theocratic Treadmill and started working to improve my standing in the group.

As for my personal observations, I noticed that the membership had increased with an abundance of African Americans, being instructed by two old white congregation overseers. They held the highest position in the congregation. There were many black men in the congregation who had reached the elder level but weren't very good at reading; something I noticed while attending service meetings. It said a lot about their education level. I know I didn't have much myself, but it seemed they had none or very little.

The Kingdom Hall seemed rife with back-biting gossip, sanctimoniousness, and mean-natured jealousy. The truth of the matter was that many of my new and old Jehovah's Witness friends were no better than those I had "in the world." I really didn't see much of a difference. From my new experience, I found that those plucked from the inner city in which I lived were no better Christians than anyone from any other faith; including myself.

As I continued to grow spiritually, I moved out of my room and in with my parents. It helped in keeping me honest because I was still weak mentally. Sex was the biggest issue I had to face; I didn't know how long I could go without it before exploding. I was used to having a warm body next to me and didn't know what to do. I needed to find something to occupy my mind, especially in the late evening hours when I was alone.

Waking up every morning and going to bed at night with the urge to perform was hard for me. Perhaps I should return to my pastime, masturbation; but forgot about the idea just as fast as it surfaced. Besides, after getting a taste of pussy, why would I do that? It was a waste of time.

My new home life was a completely different atmosphere from what I had experienced in the past; most of the time, I found myself alone. During the day, Dad was working and Mom was out "auxiliary pioneering" in field service. Most of my siblings had long moved out, and the remaining ones were still in high school.

I had just finished the CETA program and was in search of employment. Not being able to find any, I started another government-paid program called OIC (Opportunity Industrial Center.) Up to this time I had made a complete turnaround as a person and considered myself happy. I also had a love for music and became a DJ. I landed a few gigs playing at Witness wedding receptions, including that of one of my siblings.

During the next six months, my mind continued to dwell intensely about sex and my body mechanics were begging for relief. What I needed was a wife. In the *Watchtower* I could find one, but the rules were fixed.

There are times when men find themselves struggling to find a mate and start a long-lasting relationship with the opposite sex. Many set out to do it for the wrong reasons and wind up paying for it dearly; I was one of those men.

To obtain a clear conception of what happened to me once marrying a Jehovah's Witness and how it was an entirely different light from being married to one who is not, I share my brief episode with you. I share this all to warn you of what may happen if you decide to step outside of the norm; the norm being hooking up with someone outside of the *Watchtower* society who already has the basic personality that you need, but instead marrying a Jehovah's Witness who does not. This is not a one-sided story in which I am totally the victim.

The unsuspecting marriage partner thinks they are marrying someone "normal" when they marry a Jehovah's Witness. Nothing could be further from the truth; here's why. The *Watchtower* society has different sets of rules compared to other faith-based organizations regarding who you can and cannot marry. Organization rules indicate that individuals should only date and marry other witnesses of Jehovah. They used Bible Scriptures in enforcing these rules, thus regulating the rank and file.

"She is free to be married to whom she wants, only in (the) Lord" (1 Cor. 7:39).

"Do not become unevenly yoked with unbelievers. For what fellowship do righteousness and lawlessness have? Or what portion does a faithful person have with an unbeliever" (2 Cor. 6:14-15).

Searching for a mate in the rank and file of the Jehovah's Witnesses was no easy task. One of the rules as a Witness was that you couldn't "shop around," meaning you couldn't court multiple partners. Courting someone and not having the intent of marriage is a serious violation. Kissing, hand holding, touching, or other signs of affection had to be kept to a minimum if allowed at all. After coming out of the so-called world and getting a good dose of what touching and intimacy was all about, I knew this was going to be a rough ride.

During a lengthy search, I came to the realization that no one seemed to be interested in me. Just coming out of the world, I wasn't that much of a catch. I was an awkward, single, poorly paid, young fellow and had very few skills. It didn't matter who I approached, I always got rejected and treated as if I had the plague or something. Perhaps I was using the wrong deodorant; or maybe they weren't interested because they were aware that I hadn't finished my probation. Perhaps I might be a (spiritual) risk to them. All in all, I was given the cold shoulder.

The truth of the matter is that many Jehovah's Witness women act as though they are Super-Christians having no faults of their own; sin-free. They claim to be the most virtuous, sagacious, cleanest women on the planet. In my attempt to find one, I had to fashion myself like many black elders who (obnoxiously) tried their best to resemble a white man. The sisters were obsessed with marrying one of them, or someone with power within the organization. Of course, I didn't do well in that department.

Failing in my attempt to date within my jurisdictions, I started searching outside of it. Every Sunday I visited different congregations in New York City and put on a phony act, acting as if I was an elder. Unlike the sisters in the New Jersey congregations, these sisters basically acted a little differently. They seemed interested in knowing who I was. The last thing I wanted them to know was that I had just been reinstated and was on probation. To get attention, I played a character. I played the character of a part-time pioneer and elder.

As I traveled back and forth to New York, I never broke my character. Thus, many were impressed with my devotion to the *Watchtower*. But for some reason, none were interested in dating; just friendship. Then it dawned on me; I didn't have a car, didn't own a home, and didn't have a full-time job and most of all, my rap didn't match my character. I believe they noticed that. That's when I thought, what's the use? The character I was playing wasn't working. I couldn't rap to Jehovah's Witness women like I did with worldly women. I had to be more of a mannequin type, showing that I was not slick or hip. Perhaps more of a nerd type of guy.

Then it happened. One Sunday afternoon en route to a Service Meeting, I spotted an attractive young lady reading a *Watchtower* magazine on the A train. I approached her and asked if she was a Jehovah's Witness. After confirming, I revealed that I was also one. Trying to impress her as I did the others, I watered down my rap and played the nerd. To my surprise, she seemed impressed. I even tried using big words to further impress her by telling her that I was a consummate part-time pioneer (my favorite line). As I brought on the charm, I complimented her, saying she was a beautiful lady. Before exiting the train we exchanged numbers, and a friendship ensued.

I began attending meetings at her congregation whenever possible; engaging her in conversation, and tried to impress her with my sagacious understanding of biblical knowledge—or lack thereof. The truth of the matter is that I had a dearth of knowledge as to what was really going on behind the walls of the *Watchtower* society. Simply put, I was most certainly distracted by my hormonal rush triggered by her outward attractions.

Now it was time to meet her family. They lived in an apartment complex in Brooklyn, New York; a crappy place. It was surrounded by run-down buildings equal to hers. On entering, the stench of urine was unbearable; it kind of knocked you in the face when you walked in. The stairway was loaded with filth and laced with garbage. It was the same horrible scene I'd witnesses while being an around-the-clock knocker in the ghettos of Jersey City. Then again, most black people who are Jehovah's Witnesses are pulled straight from the ghetto, so it didn't bother me as much.

Once entering her apartment, I was in shocked to see that her family was living in filth. From the kitchen to the living room the stench was completely overpowering and repulsive. In her mother's bedroom, boxes were stacked as high as the ceiling. It resembled someone suffering from hoarding tendencies. I found the bathroom to be un-sanitized and in complete filth. For example, the bathroom floor and bathtub had years of grime and funk everywhere, with cockroaches running amok. There were more rings around the bathtub than around the planet Saturn.

The first question that came to mind was, how could she take a bath or shower in that filthy tub? The shower curtains were full of mildew. I will never forget that yucky sink and toilet. Toothbrushes were stained with dried-up toothpaste and the soap dish was loaded with little pieces of soap and dripping soap scum; it was gross. The toilet looked like a way station for lost souls. I was most certainly not sitting my ass on that filthy toilet seat.

When I was coming up we were poor, but were raised to keep a clean house. We washed walls, scrubbed floors, and steam-cleaned the carpets at least once a week. Her home was just plain ridiculous. I wanted to address the issue but decided to keep my mouth shut. I put on a happy face around everyone and hid my real feelings to remove any doubt that I didn't approve of their living conditions.

Before leaving her home, she offered an explanation about the condition of the apartment, blaming it on other family members who weren't Jehovah's Witnesses; they didn't care about keeping the place clean. Staring into her lovely eyes, I tried compensating her beauty for the condition of the apartment by changing the subject; but in the back of my mind, her living conditions were unacceptable. At that time in my life, I still had a mighty sex drive, and the lack of physical intimacy controlled much of my thought process. Therefore, I wasn't much concerned about her faults, so we moved on.

Once permanent contact had been established and mutual interest ascertained, we began dining out with other members of her congregation. I remember always having to have a chaperone sitting next to us, hanging on our every word. We were very rarely alone, but at times we managed to slip away and have some privacy. That's when our hand-holding, kissing, and other physical contact began; and it lit up my fire! I wasn't sure if I could handle my sexual urges in a Christ-like manner with her. This was the ultimate test to see if I'd really repented from my sins and if I was truly dedicated to Jehovah.

After introducing her to my family, I was afraid that the truth about who I really was would be revealed. That's when I dropped the character I was playing. At first I was afraid to let her know about my rocky past. Also, if I didn't reveal it, she might consider it a violation of trust and be wary of marrying me. I was also afraid she would treat me the same way I had been treated by women in my congregation, but I was wrong. She showed complete support for me and congratulated me for returning to Jehovah's organization.

Six months later we were engaged to be married. I had successfully finished the OIC program and landed a job working for a brokerage firm in New York. It was a full-time position, which helped me save the money needed for our wedding. I believed that Jehovah was blessing me for rejoining his organization and I was happy with that.

Then things started going downhill. As it started getting closer to our wedding date, my eyes became more open and I started seeing the other side of her. That's when I started harboring doubts about marrying her. It didn't mean that I had cold feet and didn't want to get married, but what it meant was, I needed to talk and express my fears and concerns. It didn't make sense to force marriage and be unhappy with our partnership several years later. Yes, I loved her, but before walking down the aisle, I wanted to make sure our relationship had those other characteristics to keep us together in sickness and in health.

What I was most concerned about was the condition of her family's apartment. It remained filthy, and for some reason, she thought that it was ok with me. Even when I found her room dirty she didn't bat an eye. To me it seemed like she never learned how to do housework and was, for lack of a better description, just lazy and nasty. This wasn't the sort of issue I could easily brush off or ignore if she was going to be my wife. This was not a question of conflicting personalities; we were Jehovah's Witnesses, and uncleanliness was unfavorable in Jehovah's eyesight, as we were taught. Before I made a drastic move, I had to take everything into consideration. I did not want to live like that for the rest of my life.

I usually keep my mouth shut, but sometimes things bear mentioning. I brought the subject up, but in a way that was loving and not judgmental. I didn't attack her verbally, belittle her, or try to crush her spirit. As I tried voicing my misgivings candidly, respectfully, upfront, and honestly, she strongly disagreed and caught an attitude. She couldn't see any further than her nose on the household disorder with the same eyes as me. From there on in we would argue constantly, and she never backed down from one. This told me that it might turn out to be a toxic relationship characterized by her refusal to listen. I couldn't speak my piece without her getting angry and flying off the handle. At times, she could be so sweet and kind; but when she wanted to have her way, it would be her way or the highway, no questions asked.

Unfortunately, as we got closer to the date, we continued to argue even more. A day never passed that she didn't challenge whatever I said or suggested to make the relationship better. She was very hardheaded and stubborn, and I wasn't taking it any more. Now I had to decide on what to do.

I didn't want to lose her, because I was in love. I had got attached to her, and my hormonal rush was at its all-time peak. Hormonal rush or no hormonal rush, I wasn't going to marry her just for that purpose. That's when I informed her that I was having second thoughts about our plans to marry, saying she wasn't ready. She disagreed and started mouthing off as usual. Now it was time to take it to the elders to coax constructive change in her or break the engagement.

We had been instructed to come to them if we had a problem we couldn't straighten out ourselves. Perhaps with their counsel, she would get the hint. Informing them was also dangerous, because breaking an engagement could result in disciplinary action, perhaps social exclusion. I was still on probation and walking a tightrope, but took a chance.

As I explained some of the conditions as to why she wasn't ready for marriage they came to her defense, saying that it might not be her, it might be me. They suggested that I had planned on bowing out of the arrangement all along, thus leading her on. They used Bible Scriptures to counsel us—mainly me—saying that I was too bossy, and that wasn't the role of a tolerant and loving husband. I held my stance and said that if she didn't change, the wedding was off. She demonstrated her displeasure and stormed out of the meeting, enraged.

The elders sat staring at me and said that I was at fault and needed to clean it up. I responded that I was only being honest about my feelings; why get married when you already know it's not going to work? I asked. They dismissed the meeting with prayer and asked me to reconsider my decision, suggesting that I needed to take it up with Jehovah in prayer.

This I did not do. Instead, I informed my parents of my decision not to carry out our plans of marriage. They suggested that I invite her and her mother over to discuss the matter and perhaps resolve it. By then I believe she had already informed her mother all the details; she seemed a little bit testy on seeing me.

The meeting didn't last fifteen minutes. Everyone focused on what I had to say. I was a bit nervous, and didn't put the blame directly on my fiancée, but said that we both weren't ready for marriage. As I continued to speak, my mother angrily cut me off saying that I thought it was all about me and that there was nothing wrong with her. Her mother got mad with the whole situation, grabbed her coat and stormed out of the house, with my fiancée following crying rivers of tears. I went after her trying to apologize but was waved off. My parents looked angrily at me, as if I was the bad guy. The pressure was so great and I felt so bad, I ran after her, gently grabbed her by the hand and against my will, I gave in saying, perhaps we could work this out. After resolving our issues, we continued with our plans for marriage.

At our wedding, we did not have the option of writing our own vows. A Jehovah's Witness elder officiated, and the vows were very old-fashioned. My new bride was basically promising to be my slave for life. The arrogant elder speaker took the opportunity to slip the *Watchtower* message in because he noticed a few visitors in the audience. Before our vows were completed, to my surprise, he made it his business to give me counsel on how to conduct myself as a Jehovah's Witness husband. Earlier, without my knowledge, my father made him aware that I was bossy and had a big ego problem. The elder remonstrated me for not being tolerant of her imperfections and rained down on me a load of Bible Scriptures saying that I must follow them as a Christian husband and head.

As he continued to remonstrate, my blood was boiling mad. What father would embarrass his son on his wedding day? Everything he told the elder was a complete lie. Now, he had bad-mouthed me in front of the whole family and friends. What he did was add fuel to my wife's hardheadedness.

Then came the wedding reception. To make a long story short, we were not rich by a long shot and had a cheap one. When my wife and I were planning our wedding reception, we wanted to keep it simple because our budget was severely stretched. Our total budget was around $2,000, so we needed to find a few ways to scrimp and save when it came to the dinner; we didn't serve alcoholic beverages.

Food is where a huge chunk of your money goes for a wedding. And since food is typically charged by the headcount, we had to plan wisely. Now we had to calculate how many chicken wings, legs, and breasts we needed to serve 60 guests and upon adding up all the expenses for our big day, we came up short; so, we had to invite fewer guests to save some dough. My parents and a few friends helped cook the chicken parts the night before, which saved us a bundle. I prayed that our guests didn't see it as the "cheap" choice to serve just chicken and rice. As much as we'd love to serve filet mignon, it just wasn't in the budget, so we had to take the economical route. You can't serve filet mignon on a chicken budget. As appetizers, we set out some cheese squares, salad, Kool-Aid, and some simple crackers. I still feel a little guilty that we had to go so cheap. All in all, everyone seemed pleased and the food tasted good.

As a Jehovah's Witness, I never realized that there were certain restrictions during the celebration. Those restrictions made everything prosaic. For instance, rice throwing, bouquet tossing, garter removal, and tin can tying were forbidden. We couldn't even toast or cheer one another with Kool-Aid. Then again, that's a part of being a Jehovah's Witness.

The first few months of our marriage went well, and all the things I was afraid would happen didn't, except for the cooking. She was essentially useless in the kitchen. She wasn't what you would call an exceptional cook. Her goal was meals that were filling, not necessarily meals that tasted good. Many nights we had roast pot instead of pot roast. However, I didn't complain. Thankfully, I was blessed with some culinary talents, which I learned from my mother, who was also gifted; otherwise, we both would have starved to death.

One thing I liked about married life is that we did things together and were invited out often. During those outings, everyone seemed to like her, especially my mother, as mentioned. The mistake we made was letting people get into our business. It started with her reporting anything that I did that wasn't scriptural to the elders of our congregation. For instance, during our third month of marriage I started taking guitar lessons, which she didn't approve of. I was always in love with the thought of being a musician. Even if I didn't make it to that point, I still wanted to learn how to play a guitar.

After getting in contact with an old school buddy who gave guitar lessons, I purchased a used guitar and started lessons with him. Twice a week he would visit our apartment and give me instructions at a small fee. This didn't go well with her because she felt that he was worldly and that I should be using that time to study the Bible with her. Meetings and theocratic life became the priority and everything else, especially including things I wanted to do, had to take a back seat. If I didn't, she would report it, and if she didn't obey me, I would report her.

Sooner or later they would pay us a visit. Right away they started giving Bible counsel on how to have a better marriage. Because of her last complaint, they focused much of their attention on me, saying I wasn't being a good Witness husband; therefore, the Holy Spirit was not operating in our home. They criticized me for taking guitar lessons, saying it was a waste of time. They felt it would take me away from my spiritual obligations; field service, book studies, Bible studies, etc., and lead to worldly enticements. I disagreed, telling them that it was a new hobby of mine and it wouldn't take me away from my service to Jehovah. As they tried to convince me I became irascible, and told them that we didn't need any help in our marriage and told them to leave. Before leaving, they suggested that we take the matter in prayer.

Shortly after they were gone, I let her know that I didn't like the idea that we let strangers in our business and suggested we handle our own business from then on in. It was none of their business how we lived our lives. But she would not agree, and continued to make complaints whenever we got into arguments. It got to the point that we were so steamed at each other, we found ourselves not speaking to one another for weeks. I continued with my guitar lessons, but soon quit to make her happy. We then resumed going to the Kingdom Hall together and the relationship got a little better.

One afternoon we were at home having lunch when one of my younger sisters, Shirley, came by to visit. She was very upset and crying. She informed me that Dad had thrown her out of the house because she had gone bowling with her best friend. Earlier, her girlfriend had been dis-fellowshipped from the Jehovah's Witnesses but both continued to remain friends afterwards. Dad wasn't having it, and disapproved of their friendship. Although a Jehovah's Witness myself, I couldn't turn my back on her as was done to me. I invited her to stay with us until the situation got straightened out. I was surprised my wife agreed; then again, although she had faults of her own, she was a kind person at heart.

After returning her home the next day I confronted my parents, asking them what sense it made throwing her into the street; home is where she belonged. I reminded them that she was not only their daughter, she was a human being. Dad objected, and we both started arguing. He was going to stand his ground no matter what I said. With a raised voice, he said, "I treat her no different than you guys. If she can't obey my rules, she must leave."

Not getting through to him, I tried appealing to Mom, saying, "She's a young lady, knows nothing about the streets, and please, don't let him do this." Mom petitioned him, suggesting that perhaps she could stay just for the night. I didn't agree with that, saying she should remain there permanently. With anger, Dad stormed into his bedroom, slamming the door behind him. Before leaving, I assured my sister that everything was going to be all right, and if not, to let me know.

I headed home, and less than twenty-four hours later, she was back at our apartment. Dad had thrown her out for good. I was infuriated with him for throwing her into the street like a dog.

From that moment on, the relationship between me and him soured. It taught me that he didn't know the first thing about Christian love and tolerance.

As for my sister, who didn't finish high school or hold a job, she was certain to face hard times just as I did when I was forced out of the home. There was no way she could compete if she wasn't complete. From there on in I vowed to help her the best I could; Jehovah's Witness or not.

As time moved on I found a second job on Wall Street in New York City teaching terminal computer operations part-time. It was a training program getting people prepared to work in various brokerage firms operating terminal computers. The company I worked for supplied me with an array of students who were looking for work and applied for the training. I let my sister know about the program and she applied and qualified, becoming one of my students. She did very well learning Wall Street language. In the computer field, and her typing skills were outstanding. After recommending her to an agency that was hiring, I was pleased when she landed her first job. Until hooking up with a boyfriend, she housed with my wife and me.

For the present she disappears from the scenes recorded in this narrative, but she will appear again before its close.

In the meantime, my wife and I started doing much better in the argument department; we didn't argue as much, and found sexier ways of enjoying one another's company. She even participated in cleaning up a little, although the cockroaches still ran rampant.

One weekend we were invited to a dinner party given by a Jehovah's Witness friend I had known for some time. That invite would change my life forever. As we indulged in pig knuckles, black eye peas and cornbread, there was a knock on the door. It was the host's brother, someone I knew very well. We actually paired up as partners while preaching years ago, when we were younger. I hadn't seen him since being dis-fellowshipped and boomeranging back into the organization. He looked weak, tired, hungry, and despondent, and projected an abject state of

93

existence. Following our host into the living room, he asked her for something to eat and for money.

She spoke with him briefly, and in doing so, was rigorous to the point of asking him to leave. He seemed embarrassed from the rejection but left without incident. I couldn't figure out for the life of me why she would treat her own brother like that. Then it hit me; perhaps he was dis-fellowshipped. My suspicions were confirmed later during the visit by the host. He had been excommunicated from the organization about the same time I was.

For the first time in my adult life, I was witnessing someone else being shunned by their own family. He was basically dismissed by her without an acknowledgment of his existence, and the treatment received was devoid of any human courtesy, mercy, or compassion. Furthermore, she was behaving in a way that I thought was deeply at odds with the Christianity we claimed to adhere to.

I was morally outraged at what I saw as the abuse of the immense psychological power this "organization" had over its members. What I had just witnessed brought back bad memories of being shunned by my family. I sat there in silence until our visit was over. On our way home, we discussed the matter and my wife defended the host's decision, saying that he was an apostate and should be shunned. We both argued somewhat and weren't on the same page when it came down to the subject of human decency and being judgmental. I reminded her what the Bible says about helping those in need:

"Share your bread with the hungry, bring the poor and homeless into your house, and clothe someone naked when you see him."

Weeks later, my mind was still focused on the incident. It was a wake-up call that something was wrong with the organization we belonged to. It was as if a cloud of dust was lifted from my mind. I could see so clearly. It was that realization that moved me to start being responsible for my own relationship with the Creator, and prompted me to do an independent study of the *Watchtower* Bible and Tract Society. I found time to research things about the society and compare what they said and what God said. While continuing with my research, I saw the repetitions, revisions of doctrinal thought, and sometimes a reversal to a previous thought. All that I had found in my research shocked me to the point of considering disassociating myself from the organization. It was now my mission to prove the *Watchtower* Bible and Tract Society was not a Christian organization; it was a very rigidly controlled group that uses social isolation and the threat of social isolation to keep people in line.

Meanwhile, I continued attending meetings and started taking more notes on every talk that was given. I paid very close attention to what was being said.

Once I put my facts together, I started having discussions with Dad and asked many questions. Since he was an elder, perhaps he could give me answers to some of the inconsistencies I saw in the organization's style of preaching the so-called truth. At that time, he did not know that I was considering disassociating myself from the organization. If he had, he wouldn't have answer any of my questions. I also thought about the consequences of what would happen to me if my family found out that I was doing a secret study on the organization. I knew that it meant they would pull away from me again; even my wife.

Weeks went by as I debated with him on the merits of the *Watchtower* society's biblically literalist interpretation of Scripture and certain quotes that didn't match with what the Bible said. He got angry when I suggested that the New World Translation might not be a valid version of God's Word. He warned me that if I continued, I would be drifting close to apostasy.

One evening, while I was attending a meeting at the local Kingdom Hall, the congregation elders wanted to have a word with me. Dad had told them about the doubts I was having about the organization. In their questioning they were belligerent, angry, and demanded an explanation. I explained that I was only trying to understand the Bible more. They wanted to know if I still considered myself a Jehovah's Witness and if so, I needed to stop questioning my father. I obliged, and was dismissed from the meeting without further incident.

Now angry at Dad's betrayal, I dug even further for information. For the time, I remained a Jehovah's Witness. I soon came to the realization that a person's belief about themselves determines almost all of their actions. Being a Jehovah's Witness made me emotionally (psychologically) dependent on the *Watchtower* leadership to define my own self-worth. Everything I believed about myself was based not on my own value as a human being created in the image of God, but on my own level of activity and social standing in the organization.

Now there were two choices I had to make. I had to decide if I wanted to let others tell me what I could think and believe, or if I was going to further investigate some of the evidence myself and reach my own conclusion. At the end of my research, I concluded that the "truth" wasn't the truth after all, and I couldn't knock on doors again. I soon disassociated myself from the organization and realized that by boomeranging, all I did was jump from the frying pan back into the fire. My transient return to the organization provided some relief from being alone and without friends, but there was no way I was going to remain with these unpleasant, sanctimonious, sick, sad people. I found it to be a dangerous and subversive organization filled with buzzwords and ridiculous theologies. I also found that keeping the truth hidden and living a lie enslaves and imprisons. For that reason, I found it ironic that Jehovah's Witnesses have co-opted the term "the truth" to use as a catch-all moniker for their beliefs and organization; ironic because I didn't find much truth there. Rather, I found the religion to be a philosophical and social trap.

Now that I had flushed out the *Watchtower*'s years of lies and replaced them with the solid foundation of truth, I had the task of informing my wife that I had disassociated myself from the organization. She already knew I was dissatisfied, and would try to get me to change my mind. The stage was set and in the back of my mind, I knew that taking this course of action would sour our relationship and our marriage could eventually end. If so, there was a chance that there was nothing I could do to turn her heart toward me.

When the time was right, I informed her of my actions. After I explained why, she was horribly fearful and wouldn't look at the evidence I presented in making my decision. I begged her to search for herself but she was convinced I had been deceived by the devil. With that note, we didn't have much to say to one another but remained together temporarily. She continued attending meetings, along with our newborn son, and had no desire to leave the Witnesses.

It is also true that I was a drag on our relationship; no Kingdom Hall, no field service, no back calls, no conventions, and no home Bible studies. Besides experiencing the hurt of knowing there was a chance of our splitting up, it was also the end of any spiritual discussions with her. I was feeling bad to cause all that hurt in her life, as it took a heavy toll on our relationship. It didn't take long for them to excommunicate me after finding out where I stood.

In the organization's rule book, I was no longer the head of our household. I had lost all rights as a Jehovah's Witness husband. For example, when it came down to saying prayer at mealtime, I was not allowed to say it. When it came down to making decisions, I was not allowed to make any.

The *Watchtower* society wrote a few articles focusing on dis-fellowshipped family member and how to handle the situation. Both of the following quotes are from *Watchtower* editions in the 1970s and 1980s.

A difficult situation arises where the husband has been dis-fellowshipped from the Christian congregation and is still in a dis-fellowshipped state. While the wife is still subject to him as her husband, yet, in harmony with the Scriptures, she can have no spiritual fellowship with him (Rom. 16:17). How might this affect the matter of prayer at mealtimes? If he insisted on praying at the meal table, the wife could not in any way acknowledge his prayer, either by a silent or an audible Amen. She can offer her own prayer silently to Jehovah while he is praying or afterward as she feels is suitable. If the dis-fellowshipped husband asked his wife to pray for the family in his presence, she would have to refuse. However, she could pray silently for herself and for the children even though he were present, but not at his direction." (*Watchtower*, April 1, 1964, pp. 203-4)

Again, the dis-fellowshipping does not dissolve the flesh-and-blood ties, but, in this situation, contact, if it were necessary at all, would be rarer than between persons living in the same home. Yet, there might be some necessary family matters requiring communication, such as legalities over a will or property. But the dis-fellowshipped relative should be made to appreciate that his status has changed, that he is no longer welcome in the home nor is he a preferred companion.

This was the mind-set of my wife and she took it to heart. It remained based on *Watchtower* principles throughout our marriage. It was heartbreaking to see how ingrained their teachings were in her, as they were in me. Often, she became abrasive and hateful toward me because I was the constant reminder that she had made a huge mistake in getting married to an "unbeliever." Now it felt like I was living with a stranger; a mindless robotic automaton of a person. She was cold, distant, calculating, and lacked the emotion and spontaneity we had before. This resulted in divisiveness in our home, which in turn led to a whole laundry list of pain for both of us.

While I still loved her unconditionally, I always said in my head, "She lays in a bed of lies," and sometimes wondered if she loved me as a husband from the start or despised me because I made a big change on things important to her. In the spirit of enquiry, I asked her many thought-provoking questions about the Society. Perhaps if she listened to subtle criticism of the organization, some things might sink in. But the harder I tried to convince her that we were involved in a cult, the more she argued and pushed me away.

The truth of the matter was that she was not skilled enough to sort out issues that led to conflicts and then effectively deal with them in a spirit of understanding and love. Like most Jehovah's Witnesses, her version of love was something that evaporates instantly once you are expelled; as in my case. I was considered an apostate, and my zealous wife couldn't hold my hand while around other witnesses, let alone continue to be "evenly yoked" when she could not even speak about anything of substance with me anymore.

As the months passed by, she maintained a shunning approach and treated me as a rabid apostate. It was like being married to your "spiritual enemy." I was only happy that she didn't evict me.

The marriage lasted longer than I thought. One year after our second child was born, I joined the New Jersey National Guard. While completing my training in Fort Benning, Georgia, my family was being torn apart by my wife's Jehovah's Witness friends. They continually warned her that her lifestyle would be threatened if she remained with me. I was a complete devil in joining the National Guard and it was against Jehovah's arrangement.

After finishing my training, I returned home to an atmosphere of pure hatred. At times, she would ask me to hide out in our bedroom whenever her Witness friends visited and stay there until they left. They weren't happy being around a dis-fellowshipped person. I tried my best to be peaceful and not upset the order of things when she had company. I put up with this inhumane treatment because I loved my family. But as the saying goes, you can kick a dog around for so long before it gets tired and turns. Well, that is just what happened, and things came to a head.

One evening my mother, along with two of my Witness sisters and their friends, paid my wife a visit. When I answered the door, they just stared at me. They acted as if I didn't belong there. I got angry and gave them a piece of my mind. My wife intervened, inviting them in. As they congregated with her, I retreated to the bedroom, angry. Things came to a head when they overstayed their visit. That night I was putting my foot down once and for all. I somehow found my voice and began to put an end to this barbaric practice of disrespect in my own home. It was time I stopped acting like a mouse and more of a man.

I asked them to leave and they just ignored me, while carrying on with their conversation. To get their attention, I grabbed their garments and tossed them in the hallway, this time telling them to get out! My mother tried to silence me, telling me to be quiet. My response was the same, everyone, get out! No one listened until my wife suggested that they leave.

Once out in the hallway, my mother displayed her anger and started arguing with me, saying, "You have no right to ask us to leave. Who do you think you are?" She was very loud.

Being afraid that my neighbors would call the police because of the commotion, I once again asked her and everyone to leave the building. That's when my sisters came to her aid. I remember one of them rushing toward me, saying, "Don't talk to her like that, you apostate!" while at the same time trying to kick me in the groin; I'm glad she missed.

In my experience, my wife was strongly advised by her friends to divorce me. The elders told her that she would need to "curtail her and the children's association" with me. This extreme, intolerant perception is justified by them because they claimed I would "shipwreck" her faith, which could ultimately lead her to leave the movement also. They also put doubts in her mind that I didn't love her because I didn't love Jehovah. Many times during our marriage I stumbled across conversations she had with these people. Usually it was when I wasn't home; as mentioned, she always had company. When returning home, I would eavesdrop before entering the apartment. I remember listening to one of her friends telling her, "He doesn't love you; Jehovah loves you." I listened to her friends using scare tactics like, she will be attacked by Satan and demons because they were latched onto me. This was the beginning of the end for our marriage.

When an expulsion happens to a married couple who are Jehovah's Witnesses, the likelihood of the marriage surviving is little to none. So, if a spouse, friend, or family member challenges the teachings or practices of the organization, the aggrieved one automatically reacts with the *Watchtower* programmed (thought-stopping) technique, which is to reject the critical person or idea as an attack from Satan.

While all of this was going on, I was very unhappy that our children had to witness the arguments, debates, and put-downs. I was hurting and felt like I was causing division for them, but I could not go along with her devotion to the Jehovah's Witnesses. On the other hand, she was worried that their blood would be on her hands at Armageddon if she remained in the marriage. Obviously, we had issues that led to our decision to split.

After finding my own apartment, I still stayed in contact with her and the kids. I had visiting rights and would pick them up every weekend. Her Witness friends, still controlling her mind, had warned her that I was trying to kidnap them. I can clearly remember her calling the police on me after not returning them home on time one weekend. Whatever she told them, they seemed angry when I answered the door. They had their hands on their firearms while questioning me. Lucky for me, the kids were standing by my side and I posed no threat to them.

In a matter of time and to my surprise, I received a letter from the local court saying that she had divorced me on grounds of separation. It was done secretly with the help of her Witness friends. She was also awarded custody of our children. When all was done, the divorce was on grounds of separation. To me the ruling wasn't fair, especially with the ruling on the kids. I most certainly didn't want them to be raised as Jehovah's Witnesses. Secondly, you can only divorce your spouse on grounds of adultery, which wasn't the case with me. Before I could challenge anything, she had remarried. Her new husband was also a Jehovah's Witness. Now I was concerned about our children and the influence her new husband would have on them in becoming *Watchtower* slaves.

Chapter 11: Here Comes the Bride

That being said, the most important thing for me was to raise them far, far away from anything Jehovah's Witness related. I didn't feel it was right to push religion on them as it was pushed on me. I also didn't want them to be indoctrinated into an organization that instructed them to judge, condemn, and hate others in the name of religion. I continued to do for them all the things I longed for as a child; Halloween, pumpkin patches, birthday parties, sports, time to run outside and be free, not stuck sitting in some Kingdom Hall listening to old, tired men telling them what to do or how they should live.

Now that they were young adults and impressionable, I continued to teach them to think for themselves, to think critically, and that while individual Jehovah's Witnesses (their mother) may be decent folks, their organization is a whirlpool of soul- and mind-sucking evil that needs to be blotted from the universe.

However, they have not grown up completely unscathed by the organization. Their mother is deeply entrenched and continues to try to convert them, even as adults. The upside is that they have not followed in her footsteps.

Once my marriage failed, my experience led me to believe that Jehovah's Witness women were no different than any other women in the world as they claim; in fact, they may be the worst in their thought process (compartmentalized thinking) and in raising children. Jehovah's Witness love can be conditional when compared to so-called worldly women. Their thoughts are not driven by their private feelings but are bound by rules from *Watchtower* objectives, which they demand to be effectively met.

Another lesson I learned was to never step into a marriage with someone just for the sake of sex, the partnership, or the image. I wanted to be loved badly, and was struggling with loneliness and lust. I was so impressed with the package that I didn't care about the contents, which I knew. The truth is that my name was not Brother Thomas, but Brother Hormone. Yes, we really clicked at times, which I felt was quite refreshing, but my driving motivation was still the same as it was when I was out

102

and about in the world; a force driven by lust and some external attributes.

I foolishly allowed myself to be yoked with an ass, and the two of us started pulling one against the other. I truly believe that my life would be completely different, and my children's life much better, had I not married a Jehovah's Witness. When two people are pulling against each other, it makes it very difficult for anything to work.

From my experience, the following are some of the sacrifices you and your family would have to make if you marry a Jehovah's Witness:

• You will be required to give up a lot of your free time in the evenings and weekends to prepare for and attend Jehovah's Witness meetings, preach door-to-door with your spouse, and conduct *Watchtower* Bible studies in the homes of potential converts.

• You are required to force your children to preach door-to-door instead of playing with non-Jehovah's Witnesses relatives and friends on the weekend. They are required to do their *Watchtower* homework in addition to school homework in the evenings, and to attend *Watchtower* meetings instead of extracurricular school activities (like music and sports).

• Both parties are required to report their monthly door-to-door time to the elders for evaluation and criticism if they think you could have done more.

• You are not allowed to celebrate your wife's, husband's, or children's birthday or holidays, such as Thanksgiving, Christmas, or Easter. You are required to turn down your non-Jehovah's Witness relatives' holiday dinner invitations.

• You will be discouraged from having oral sex as married couples.

• You will not be allowed to vote, salute the flag, or defend your nation against attacks by other nations.

• You are required to let your children die rather than give them a needed blood transfusion.

- You will not be allowed to question or doubt any of the beliefs of Jehovah's Witnesses with your spouse or elders.

- If your spouse or children leaves the faith, you will be required to shun them, no matter how much you love them, by avoiding unnecessary communication with them, refusing to greet them, or invite them to family gatherings.

- Being married to a Jehovah's Witness does not ensure a happily ever after.

If your goal is to have a marriage free from the control of legalistic men and one that places the teaching of the Bible as supreme in your home, you will need to seek elsewhere for a blessing; not the Jehovah's Witnesses. If you need to find a Bible-based church and are looking to marry, the Jehovah's Witness organization is the last place on earth to find that luxury. They are one of the most ridiculous of cults, and they do have a HUGE impact on breaking up families, as they did mine.

# Chapter 12

# *As One Dead*

Anyone who has been cut off and disowned by their family in the name of religion knows it is one of the worst things that can happen to a human being. When I think of someone who has been disowned I picture a drug addict, a murderer, a serial killer, or a prostitute. I can't imagine anything a person could do short of these things that would make their parents and family be anything but supportive and caring. Shunning/Disfellowshipping is sick; the ultimate fuck you to someone; worse if they are family. *Evil* is the only word that can be applied to such draconian practices of disowning family members.

The negative experience of leaving the Jehovah's Witnesses was in all the temporal immediate circumstances. You know that a decision you make is going to make you lose everybody you have known, everybody who is important to you, everything that is of value to you. The people you know and love who are your spiritual family, spiritual teachers, spiritual mothers and fathers, sisters and brothers, children, people that I was close to; this one decision to leave was going to make them treat me as though I were dead.

As the years dragged on, the shunning took its toll; especially with regard to my mother. My heart couldn't take or accept the fact that she refused to speak to me, even when I saw her in public. She had embarrassed me several times in front of my friends and it was hard to take.

For example, I was working as a security guard at the local hospital and she was there to visit one of my sisters who was having foot surgery. Anyone entering the building had to get a pass and then get checked in by me and my coworkers. As she approached me, she said nothing, just looked the other way and proceeded to the elevator. My coworker knew her and asked about the "dis." After I explained the Jehovah's Witness rules, he shook his head in disbelief, saying his mother would never do such a thing. I had never been so embarrassed like that in my life. This is only one example of her utter disdain for me; there's not enough room in this book to name all the others.

My father shared the same pulse. He was very distant and a complete moron. I hated the fact that he would never inform me whenever Mom was sick. It was always after the fact, and reported by someone else in the family months or years later. I remember being told by one of my friends that she had been knocked out in a car accident, but I was never notified or informed by him.

Then came the retirement party. When my father retired from his job as a truck delivery driver, Mom gave him a surprise retirement party. She thought it was ok to invite most of her Jehovah's Witness friends, but not me. Although he was a cruel and difficult man, he put food on the table for many years and I didn't have a problem with thanking him for that. Most of my relatives who were not Jehovah's Witnesses were invited, as well as my Witness siblings. After being excluded, it sank in that I meant nothing to her; I can remember the anguish that I was in, and I felt a certain amount of antipathy toward her. She didn't care one bit about important family events such as this; she was entirely apathetic.

Even when it came down to the death of a relative; many whom I cared for and loved have passed away without me ever seeing them again. I was not good enough to be informed, as they concluded that my level of love for them was not important. I could have at least been given the opportunity to pay my respects. Then again, neither parent ever called or texted me in my entire life. The same goes for my Jehovah's Witness siblings; I meant nothing to them. Only when they needed something; and when they got it, they angered me by saying I love you. It's pure hypocrisy to say you love a person on one hand, but treat them as if they were dead on the other.

I had already figured out what kind of love they had for me. It's the love you feel for a dog when you can get them to do things you say and then come to you wagging their tail and showing affection. But that same dog can get tossed out of the house and onto the street a moment later if it did something not agreed with.

Not longing for any more of this heartbreak and total despicable disrespect, I decided to move out of town and start a new life of my own. In 1985 I moved to South Jersey, a place where no one knew me, just about sixty miles from home. I didn't want to move too far from my kids because I wanted to be in their lives, naturally.

Now away from all the haters, I felt a little sigh of relief. But my mother constantly stayed on my mind most of the time. I was worried because as she was getting older, I was afraid that I would never get the chance to see or speak to her again.

I especially thought about her when the holidays came. Throughout the years, those were the days I was most lonely, and wished she'd pay me a visit. But then again, that was wishful thinking on my part.

During those years, I often sat alone in the darkness of my apartment feeling depressed, sometimes accompanied by a few six-packs of beer. To me, every holiday was a reminder that I was as one dead. It seemed that I had been thrown into a virtual prison. My feelings were hurt, ego damaged, and at times I felt sorry for myself with thoughts of suicide, as in the past. I often had to keep reminding myself that I had children and that wouldn't be a good idea, so I just drank the pain away. The truth of the matter is that shunning really is a slow, legal way to kill someone. If it doesn't kill you physically, it surely does emotionally.

Fast forward to 2004; I received a phone call from one of my sisters informing me that a fire started in our parents' home and that our mother was hurt as she tried to escape the flames. When all was said and done, she was treated for her wounds and released from the hospital. The fire did great damage to their home and they were not allowed to return.

At that time, I had just bought my first home and offered them a place to stay free of charge. Perhaps this was a chance for us to be reconnected. Having them both living with me would have been the first time they would have seen some of my outstanding accomplishments in life, and perhaps change their minds about me. Nothing could be further from the truth. I was living in a dream to think this would happen. They couldn't have cared less about anything I did or accomplished if I wasn't a Jehovah's Witness.

They rejected my offer, and instead took up residence in a small basement apartment of a home of one of their Jehovah's Witness friends. In the end, their actions enraged me all over again at the outright shunning. It was also another reminder that I was nothing to them. I never wanted to believe that, but this time it really sank in; but the shunning does not end there.

In 1983, I wrote my parents a letter pertaining to the subject matter of shunning and brutality. I criticized them for not giving support to our family, and I specifically mentioned my sister Shirley's name who will appear in this narrative later. I did not get a response from that letter.

The trauma and drama in our family continued as the years passed by; father against son, son against father, brother against brother, sister against brother; a never-ending story. We were all drifting further and further apart and getting much older.

One of the true by-products of being a Jehovah's Witness is that it leads them to make it more difficult for others, and for no reason that makes any sense. All people face the same fundamental human problems of loving, of suffering, and of fulfilling human aspirations. My Jehovah's Witness family are no different. Although they claim to be above the rest, they are not. Their attitude toward me was one of the most crucial stumbling blocks that I experienced and one of the reasons trying to communicate with them was so frustrating.

The only way to try to resolve this divide, was for me to pen a letter and send it out to the entire family in an effort of opening their eyes to a different resolve and come together. Abraham Lincoln said it well: "A house divided against itself cannot stand...no matter how much you try to fake it!" Unfortunately, I could not open their eyes with that letter. The problem of stubbornness has hampered and stomped out that effort, so I hope that God will deliver them and remove the scales from their eyes.

There were many days I walked a tightrope between my own sanity and stability, sometimes falling into states of desperation, grief, and instability over my hopeless situation and how I was treated. At times, I felt vindictive; is it any wonder I still feel like picking up a grenade launcher and firing a few rounds at more than a few Kingdom Halls? But then again, as I mentioned earlier, two wrongs don't make a right—and it's against the law. I find the only means of escaping this type of hurt and shunning is to live and to find peace that comforts the depths of my very soul.

# Chapter 13

## *My Beloved Sister Shirley*

Before completing this book, as mentioned in an earlier chapter, my sister Shirley would return to the narrative. What a wonderful woman she was. She had a smile about a mile wide and for a good reason, it was simple, straightforward, and most important sincere. I an attest to that because during our struggles we did manage to spend some time together laughing and clowning. For example, she loved New York City and the petty arcades located all throughout 42$^{nd}$ street and 8$^{th}$ avenue. Shirley was her name, the pin-ball machine was her game. We loved competing against each other, and it was a blast! I remember showing her my skills at the game; bragging and saying, "You'll feel my power now.' She would die laughing at my clowning around and making funny faces as I turned the machine out. I remember feeling the joy in seeing her laugh. Sometimes it was me, my girlfriend, her and her boyfriend out having a good time. She had a benign personality and was pleasant to be with. Even when it came down to her best friend who was a Jehovah's Witness that had been disfellowshipped, she didn't disown or shun her as instructed by our parents. She made the decision to remain friends with her for life and it cost her dearly; as shall be explained. Like me, she also had the gift of gab. She was gregarious, garrulous and affable. I thought I always had the last word…she had the last 5000 ☺ in short, she was a remarkable person.

Another thing about her is that she was a basic needs person. She was not selfish, aggressive or driven by destructive forces. She loved observing wild animals, birds, plants and other natural phenomena. She also wanted to be loved and she wanted to love, that was one of her most basic needs. When she was thrown out at the age of eighteen, the most important nourishment she required during her development went missing in action, and it continued for a while. That nourishment is the feeling that she is communicated with and that she is loved. That there is a person or persons who love her, who communicate to her the feeling that another person is profoundly interested in her welfare, who is there to support and encourage her in her development and to offer her all the assistance and stimulation she requires. Unfortunately, at that time in her life, that didn't happen with her, although she was worth all the love she had been denied.

Finding love finally came her way when she met the love of her life. Eventually they would become engage and would soon marry. They planned their wedding day and had decided to marry and settle in the state of Florida. I knew from that moment on, I would miss her once gone.

As her wedding day approached, she was worried that our father would not walk her down the aisle or that our mother would not attend the event. Since her fiancé was not a Jehovah's Witness and she was disfellowshipped, the answer was obvious. Therefore, I stepped in to replace him and she was happy about that.

From the beginning, the stage was set where there would never be a father of the bride dance if the husband was not a Jehovah's Witness. I was afraid that she would break down and bawl on her wedding day because she didn't have the special mother-daughter moments. But then again, she wouldn't have those moments even if they were still in her life.

She sadly approached me, worried about being embarrassed because our family was nowhere to be found. The only one giving her the respect she deserved were me and three other non-Jehovah's Witness sisters. I simply told her that she should go mingle with her husband's side of the family and try to enjoy her best day. I could never forget the expression of her sadness on her face. As much as her new husband loved her, it didn't replace the feeling of having a mom, dad, uncles, and aunts around you on that day. No one was there to ask her how she was doing or to

111

congratulate her after the wedding. She had been embarrassed for no reason.

I saw the hurt in her eyes and it wasn't pretty. Our family had sent the message that she was nothing, unworthy of praise and honor on her most special day. As she walked away, I felt hatred for my parents, especially Dad. What he did was shame her name by not walking her down the aisle; I silently cursed him. Then I thought about our mother. How could she not attend her own daughter's wedding? How could she live with herself or sleep at night without having a guilty conscience?

Tragically, just five years into their marriage, her husband died. Once again she was all alone, but managed to find someone to fill the void. The relationship was an abusive one, and it all went downhill from there.

Going back to July of 2010, I received a phone call from a family member informing me that she was admitted to the hospital and was in the intensive care unit and in critical condition. The hospital was in West Palm Beach Florida. I immediately prepared myself for the trip.

Upon my arrival at the hospital, I entered the intensive care unit and it was heartbreaking viewing my sister's condition. She looked like she had been living under a bridge for a long time. Her hair was unkempt and she looked malnourished, but she was still alive, barely. Her live-in boyfriend was nowhere to be found for questioning. Over the years of her living with him, he was very abusive. The evidence was staring me right in the face. I wanted to kick his ass, and bad, for letting her deteriorate into such a morbid condition without letting the family know. A few years earlier I traveled to Florida to confront him after she reported his abuse; I should have buried his ass then.

By now her vital statistics were low and she had lost most of her faculties. She lay in a comatose state. The doctors were very concerned about her condition, and wanted my parents to decide on what to do. They had suggested two things; hospice or a nursing home. Even though her situation looked bleak, the doctors gave her a fifty/fifty chance of survival because of her young age of forty-seven.

Since my parents were the legal guardians (she had no children or a living will), they had to make the decision on whether she would live or die. Because of their faith and the rules pertaining to life and death, I was afraid they would sentence her to death. In my lifetime, I had seen many of my friends die because their Jehovah's Witness parents made wrong decisions in preserving their lives (especially on blood issues).

To my surprise, my father decided to take a vote to put her into hospice or a nursing home. When all was said and done, everyone agreed to put her in a nursing home. I was happy that there was a chance she would recover and be removed from the intensive unit.

When it came down to her aftercare, I wasn't so happy. My parents decided to put her in a nursing home in Florida instead of New Jersey where they lived. I objected because I thought it would be a complete recipe for disaster. She was vulnerable; 1,500 miles from home, with no family infrastructure nearby and an abusive boyfriend who we didn't know that much about; and at least someone could physically check up on her closer to home. My suggestions were denied and the stage had been set for her recovery, minus her family.

After returning home I was very concerned about her welfare, with no one being around her to give an accurate report. So in August of the same year I went back to check up on her, as she was still hospitalized. By that time, she had been transferred out of the intensive care unit and placed in a regular room; something I was happy about. However, once entering her room, all indications were that no one had been there to look after her well-being. Not even her live-in boyfriend had come to visit. It was so sad to see her laying there without any kind of support from anyone.

I looked around and noticed that she had not eaten the food given her. She most certainly needed someone to help her to eat because of her weak condition. I also noticed that she was doing a little better than before. She was conscious, and conversed with me briefly, but was somewhat delusional and paranoid. She thought our parents were on their way to visit her and asked if I saw them in the hospital lobby. Knowing this not to be true, I changed the subject to something less stressful. Earlier, her doctor had instructed her to keep moving her legs for better circulation, something I noticed she was doing, and encouraged her to keep up the effort if she wanted to get better.

In the last hour of my visit, I made her promise me that she would eat her food and if she couldn't, request some assistance from the nursing staff. She also asked me the most heart-breaking question that I couldn't answer; big brother, am I going to die? And that just about blew me away. I quickly changed the conversation and reminded her that if she didn't eat her food, she wouldn't get better. Before heading back to the hotel, I spoke with her nurse and doctor about her condition and her lack of nutrition. They assured me that they would do all they could do to help her.

That evening, while sitting in the hotel lobby, every detail of that afternoon visit remained etched in my memory; especially her asking me if she was going to die. The thought of her care raced across my mind time after time and time again. There was only so much the doctors and nursing staff could do for her. Someone from the family needed to be there to make sure she was eating and getting the right medications.

Earlier, when I'd arrived at the hospital, the doctors informed me that no one came to visit her in the month that she had been hospitalized; that's why I was worried. Now the time for me to leave was approaching and I didn't want to leave her to fend for herself under those circumstances. For me, doing so became a source of unspeakable guilt.

At the end of the day she was on her own, and thus all went downhill from that moment. The following month she was admitted into a nursing home to begin her rehabilitation. Just a few weeks later, she signed herself out without finishing it and returned to her live-in abuser; something I had warned against. He called one of my sisters saying that she hadn't eaten in 14 days; was bed-ridden and extremely malnourished. She then called the police, fire and rescue squad in West Palm Beach, to inform them as to what was taking place. Once arriving and seeing her condition, they took her to the hospital where she was admitted in critical condition and placed into the intensive care unit. Our parents were informed and got in touch with the hospital over the phone. Once the doctors briefed them, they made the decision to place her in the hospice unit. I would hear nothing about their decision until a sibling called to inform me on New Year's Eve. By then she had been in hospice for two weeks. I was on my way.

Once arriving, I headed straight to the hospice unit and there she was; my loving sister. It was truly a sad sight to see. She was half the size she was when I saw her in August, just some 125 days prior. She looked as if she was already dead. I soon realized it was only after two weeks of being there with no life support, meaning food or water, that her condition deteriorated. Still, her eyes were open, and she recognized me. She was so weak and frail she couldn't even move her limbs or talk. I called her name and told her that "big brother" was here (that's what she used to call me). For one reason or another, I just couldn't get it into my head that when a person is placed into a hospice unit, they are there for one reason; to die. Perhaps I just didn't want to believe that; but now I was faced with that reality.

The next morning, as I returned to the hospital it was a different scene. She was totally unresponsive and comatose. I decorated her room with the most lovable things I could find and afford. Later that day I contacted the hospital chaplain and asked him to bless her. He kindly took out his Bible and read James 5 verse 14:

"Is any one of you sick? He should call the elders of the church to pray over him and anoint him with oil in the name of the Lord."

He then anointed her with oil and prayed earnestly for her. We thanked him dearly, and he mentioned that he would be around if needed. The nursing staff was also very kind and let me sty in the same room with her for the next full week. The room was equipped with a comfortable sofa couch. Now I would be by her side up until the very end. There was no way I was going to let her die alone. It would be the most disrespectful act of all time.

As the days went by, I kept a log on her condition and medication all the way up until her final moment. It was a very difficult time for me but I did my best to show her love and comfort, as did the nursing staff and doctors. After staying by her side for about a week, her vital statistics started dropping and I knew that it was only a matter of time. I felt down-hearted and unhappy all day long, and when I lay down upon the small sofa couch that night, my heart was oppressed with such a load of grief, it seemed that it would break. My cup of sorrow was full to overflowing; it was hard to sleep that night.

I got through the night and was about to bid my sister farewell. I must ask the reader to go back with me to chapter nine, to follow the letter I wrote to the family; to learn the effect it didn't produce, and that while I was alone and despairing in the hospice unit, the goodness of that letter fell on deaf ears.

Throughout the morning and afternoon hours I sat by her bedside, watching her ever fading respirations. Continually brushing her hair with my hand, I apologized to her for no one being there and asked her to forgive me for not saving her life.

The day before she passed, I sang a song to her, "You'll Never Walk Alone" written by Richard Rodgers; it was completely fitting:

> When you walk through a storm hold your head up high
> and don't be afraid of the dark. At the end of the storm
> there's a golden sky and the sweet silver song of the
> lark. Walk on, through the wind walk on, through the
> rain. Though your dreams be tossed and blown. Walk
> on, walk on, with hope in your heart and you'll never
> walk alone. Walk on, walk on with hope in your heart
> and you'll never walk alone. You'll never walk alone.

That Saturday morning, a group of doctors came in to check up on her condition and before they left, I thanked them for caring for her. She was now about to reach the end of her earthly journey and lay down to her final rest without kith nor kin to mourn for her before that hour. Before her final moments, I spoke to her about everything. It is said that when a person is comatose, they can still hear. I began telling her that it was ok to go and that I loved her. Although she was unable to reach out for me while on her deathbed, I hugged her and felt her spirit respond. To stand there holding her hand, knowing I was helpless in changing her condition, and watching her fade into death, was one of the most devastating moments of my life. Watching her take her last breath was like watching a butterfly fall asleep, its wings fluttering progressively more slowly until they become motionless. It was with tears and a heavy heart, not many minutes later, that I watched her die.

At 4:13 p.m. on January 22, 2011, she was pronounced dead. It was very peaceful, quiet, and beautiful. After informing the family, I got down on my knees and read Psalms 23 verses 1-6.

"The Lord is my Shepherd; I shall not want."

Viewing her skeletal body, I witnessed the same facial expression of disappointment and sadness etched on her face that she'd had when times were hard for her. Feeling empty and worthless, I felt somewhat relieved when the nursing staff came in to offer their condolences. They informed me that they had called the funeral home, saying I could stay with the body until they arrived.

Before her body was removed, I looked for the last time upon her lifeless form. I'm only happy that having me by her side could have made her journey from this world a little easier. Nothing eases the mind like having someone by your side. Whether we're in a peaceful moment or a crisis, praying and sharing love can help us feel understood, validated, and supported as we navigate through this life. As we transition in our journey, we come to realize how precious and rare soul connections are.

After her removal I was devastated and needed emotional support, but there was no one there to give it. I now had the task of arranging for the next step. This had to be done because if I wasn't there, she may have wound up in potter's field, so I had to move fast.

I spent the next two weeks in Florida and made all the necessary arrangements that our parents requested over the phone. Upon their request, she was cremated, and her ashes sent to them in the State of New Jersey. It was a long journey that I shall never forget.

At the end of the day, it all boils down to one thing, "judgment." The judgment is brutal!

# Chapter 14

## *Shirley's Memorial*

Two months after my sister's death, my father prepared a memorial for her. I drove to New Jersey still sadden by her death. My heart felt truly ripped out and I was shut down emotionally for a long during this time. Now I had to face those in my family that I haven't seen for over 30 years who were still Jehovah's Witnesses. It was going to be an awkward moment. Before this time, I had never been to a memorial given by Jehovah's Witnesses and didn't know what to expect.

Once arriving at the service, all the family members were in attendance with an exception of a younger brother that was incarcerated. Before the memorial began, programs were handed out and after close examine, I didn't see my name on the program. I thought that since I was the last person to see her alive, they would give me a few minutes to say something in her behalf. I was not afforded that luxury. I was told that I was forbidden to say anything because of being disfellowshipped and it wouldn't be appropriate. Yet, no one in the family that was Jehovah's Witnesses got up and said nothing in her behalf; it was very confusing.

After accepting this, I sat quietly during the service. It was indeed a loveless and sterile affair, with little in the way of comfort and solace. After the service I remember my older brother approaching me with an outstretched hand. I didn't want to shake it because he had shunned and abandoned me for 30 plus years; but out of respect, I shook his hand. After that, he said nothing; no conversation, no interest in how my life was going. Then he wanted to take photos of us together. In my mind I'm asking why? Why would he want to take pictures with me but rejected my love and friendship over the years? My older sister, who has shunned me even longer (40 plus years); the one who kept me off the memorial program, didn't bat an eye my way; neither did her husband or children. One of my younger sisters followed in her footsteps. Her entire family rolled their eyes at me as I passed by them. The few brothers and sisters that were no longer Jehovah's Witnesses had very little to say; can't figure that one out.

My mother on the other hand did approach me and said, "thank you for going down and taking care of Shirley, you saved daddy a trip." Of course, I stood there in disbelief that she would say such a thing. After that she just ignored me the rest of the time. My father remained silent not even looking my way. It was sad that the whole witness side of the family was devoid of natural affection that day. The way they treated me was despicable! The fact remains that relations between our family, were so acrimonious that each refused to acknowledge the presence of the other. Yet, I was pleased that my two children and granddaughter gave their support. They took a sad song and made it better.

It has now been four years, and the fourth anniversary for my beloved sister has now passed. For me, forgetting about her feels a lot worse than remembering the pain. No family member has planned any type of a memorial service or candlelight vigil to honor her name. No one has reached out to someone else still grieving the loss via letter, card, phone call, or email. My parents have not yet built a memorial with portraits, personal items, and objects that remind siblings and relatives of her when visiting their home. They have her ashes hidden in a drawer. They have no idea what to do with them, as they don't have any loving feelings to do something respectful with them. So, there they sit; in a box.

There is an answer to all of this, and the answer lies within me. Every year I have an anniversary ceremony for her. While I do not have her ashes, I light candles and pray for her and to her. Not a year goes by without me doing so. I invited my non-Jehovah Witness siblings to join each year, but to no avail.

As time moved on, I had to find a new family, one that could help me release some of the pain that I still carried. A family who wouldn't judge me for what I did or didn't do. I soon found the nerve and entered a house of worship. Having no prior church experience, I didn't know exactly what to do as I entered. I simply followed what everyone else did; standing, singing, greeting each other, etc. When the preacher invited all to approach the altar, I remained in my seat because I didn't know what an altar was or what I was supposed to do. I certainly didn't want to embarrass myself. I was amazed to see people on their knees praying, weeping, and giving praise. They could express their feelings without being controlled or relegated to their seats as I was accustomed to when I was a Jehovah's Witness.

When the choir began singing, I began to cry uncontrollably as it felt so comforting to me. This was most certainly my new home. I began attending regularly and enjoyed the "true" love and kindness being shown by most everyone. For the first time in my life, I felt that I wasn't being judged by others, and found a relationship with God. There are many storms in life, and there is scarcely anyone who has not experienced some degree of misery and needed some support. I have found that support and the memory of my misery carries with it the memory of loving care I receive from those in my new family.

# Chapter 15

## *The Final Act*

In June of 2014, I was made aware through one of my ex-Jehovah's Witness sisters that Mom had taken sick and was constantly in and out of the hospital. Over the years, whenever she got sick and was hospitalized, I was never notified until months after she left the hospital. This time around it was every other week that I was notified, which sent up red flags. I immediately bought train tickets to go pay her a visit.

Over the years, I have never been invited to her home, as mentioned earlier, and I wasn't sure if I would be accepted. If I went to visit her against her will, I might force her into a position in which she would have to compromise her convictions or turn me away; or there might be a confrontation and a bad scene with my Jehovah's Witness siblings or her Jehovah's Witness friends if they were there visiting. Nevertheless, I had to take that chance. I needed to find out for myself why she was always sick and in and out of the hospital.

Once arriving in town, I picked up my son to bring him along with me. I didn't think they would not accept me as long as I had him with me. After driving to her home, I was surprised to see that one of my non-Witness brothers was outside in front of her home along with his son and girlfriend. I was happy to see that, and it made me feel less pressure. He was also dis-fellowshipped as I was, and if they accepted him, perhaps they would accept me. To my surprise we were invited in, and no one mentioned us being dis-fellowshipped. After the initial greetings, we all sat down in the living room, where we engaged in conversation about her health.

The last time I'd seen or heard from her was during my sister's memorial service four years before, and she looked healthy. This time around, it wasn't the same story. I was shocked to see that she had lost tremendous weight and was frail. This made me fearful and afraid for her. Looking over at Dad, who sat there quietly, I wanted to ask him why he didn't inform me about her condition; something I didn't do, because I already knew the answer. For the next few hours I tried to milk her for information about her health and the medication she was taking, but she offered very little, changing the subject constantly. She was more engaged with my brother's girlfriend and their girly talk and paid little attention to me. That's when I decided to just sit and be quiet. All in all, it was a pleasant visit and after leaving, I didn't realize that that would be the last time I would see her alive.

A year and a half had passed when I was telephoned by one of my sisters (an ex-Witness) who lives in the same state to tell me Mom was sick again and in and out of the hospital. Once again, everything was after the fact. She had been sick for the last four months, and Dad wouldn't even pick up the phone to let me know and it enraged me once again. From there on in, the only information was coming from her. Dad confided in her more than me, which always puzzled me because she is also dis-fellowshipped.

In August of 2014, my sister called to say that Mom had been placed in a nursing home after leaving the hospital. During her hospital stay she was being treated for asthma. Of course, I had no idea that she was even in the hospital, as I was told by no one. She also informed me that the nursing home didn't look sanitized and they were having a meeting that Monday morning to discuss other options. During our conversation, I mentioned that we might be able to get her into a different place and made some suggestions on how it could be done. I then outlined it in the letter and sent it to her through email. I asked her to print it out and take it with her to the meeting and give it to our father. When all was said and done, I didn't get a response, so I had to try to find a different plan; perhaps her organization could help her, so I thought.

Unlike other religions, the Jehovah's Witnesses don't take care of their elderly and they don't have retirement or nursing homes for them. You would think that at least they would send her a nurse or pay her medical bills for her loyal service to the organization. It's so sad that she put all her eggs in one basket; the Jehovah Witness basket of lies and deceit.

A few weeks had passed when I was informed by my sister that she had caught pneumonia while at the nursing home and was hospitalized. Everything went downhill after that moment. While being treated for pneumonia and asthma, she suffered a mild heart attack. In the few weeks that she was receiving treatment, she suddenly took a turn for the worse and on Wednesday, October 14, 2015, at 2:14 p.m., she was pronounced.

Ironically, and sadly enough, the curtain had gone down on the final act of my family. For me, it would be the final act of a long-fought battle for love and acceptance. For many years I used to worry that she might die before we ever had any kind of understanding or resolution between us. I was always holding my breath, knowing I would soon be getting that call; either to come to her deathbed or to a funeral, especially as she was approaching her mid-eighties.

The disbelief of her sudden death and trouble connecting my emotions to the facts about her told me that I had suddenly hit rock bottom with the truth at last. We were not going to resolve our differences; time had run out. I tried visiting her while she was in the hospital, but because of flooding issues in my state, my method of transportation was halted; that was the week she passed.

Sadly, her death was the resolution for me. I had treated her with as much kindness as I could muster. I had always imagined a scenario where we reached closure and reconciliation, where she might truly understand what happened, be remorseful, and apologize fully, and where I would accept that apology. A pipe dream is what it was. I know I tried everything to make that happen, but I failed because I couldn't do her part.

As I struggled with trying to get her to accept me, I came to the realization that she had disowned me so many times I wouldn't be able to count them. I gave up on her a while ago, calmly, without a fight, probably because I already knew how hopeless it

was. She had been told by the *Watchtower* society that I was part
of the antichrist, and that was one of her reasons for abandonment.

"Apostates are considered and treated worse than adulterers,
pedophiles and murders. Apostates must not be spoken to and
their books must not be read. They must be "loathed" and "hated",
are said to eat from the "table of demons." (*Watchtower*, October
1, 1993, p. 19)

"True Christians share Jehovah's feelings toward such
apostates; they are not curious about apostate ideas. On the
contrary, they "feel a loathing" toward those who have made
themselves God's enemies, but they leave it to Jehovah to execute
vengeance." (*Watchtower*, November 1, 1993, p. 19)

"But remember, in this case Jehovah is the One who tells us
in his Word what to do. And what does he say about apostates?
Avoid them" quite mixing in company with them and never
receive them into your homes or say a greeting to them."
(*Watchtower*, March 15, 1986, p. 13)

"Such ones {apostates} willfully abandoning the Christian
congregation thereby become part of the 'antichrist."
(*Watchtower*, July 15, 1985, p. 31)

God's loving people? I think not. With quotes like these, I
didn't stand a chance with her. Unconditional love does not exist
in the Jehovah's Witness organization. They have forever
encouraged disconnection. I've already mourned never having a
relationship with her, and there's nothing left to mourn. It was like
grieving for the living, a difficult and painful daily process that I
think was much harder than staying sober. I had this constant
mortal emotional wound, like a huge gaping hole that never
closes, and it never healed completely. If it was physical, I would
have died from it a long time ago.

The relationship ball was in her court, but she never hit it back
to me. She withheld love, affection, and support for most of my
adult life. She never made any effort to be serious, listen,
communicate, show emotion, empathy, or regret. She had
manipulated my genuine care for horrible selfish gain and very
often at my expense, physically, mentally, emotionally, and

financially. Living my life wanting what she was incapable of giving me and hoping she would see the light and do her own inner work was depending on a hope that was never going to happen.

I don't think I'll ever get over the isolation she made me feel. I didn't isolate her; her beliefs kept her from a relationship with me. She had 62 years to build a relationship with me but didn't. She shunned me for the final 34 years of her life.

Perhaps I should hate or be angry with her, but I'm not. I feel sorry for her because she was a victim of brainwashing, but I don't feel sorry for her at my expense anymore. She did just as much damage as my father did. I know life is unfair, and mothers are not always what we want them to be. I know that I am worthy of so much more than she ever offered me. I love her, miss her, and find relief in knowing that this dysfunctional dance is finally over.

My final message to my beloved mother: Mama…I just want you to know that you are always in my prayers for as long as I live. Your loving son, who misses you so much.

Dad made the decisions to have services for Mom at the local Kingdom Hall. I, along with others, were in opposition to this decision. In the past, I had vowed never to enter a Kingdom Hall ever again. I most certainly did not want to enter the place that had excommunicated me, ruined my life, and most of all, prohibited my mother from having anything to do with me. I felt the service should be held in a public place; perhaps a community center or a funeral home.

Nevertheless, he carried out his decision and had the wake and funeral one half-hour apart. I found this odd and objected, because a wake is usually held in the evening. Having the arrangements one-half hour apart was not enough time and for a very good reason: People offer their sympathy to the grieving family. It gives the family an opportunity to hear from family and loved ones when they're prepared to deal with it and in the grieving mind-set. One half-hour is not enough time when so many people are offering their condolences.

I offered to provide any suggestions if needed, such as options for the obituary, seating arrangements, or the amount of time available for the ceremony. I also wanted to be in charge of choosing five men, including myself, to attend her casket. We would be charged with carrying her coffin from the Kingdom Hall and at the cemetery, and it would have been an honor; yet I was still turned down. I was completely shut out of making any arrangements whatsoever. Perhaps my being dis-fellowshipped had something to do with Dad keeping me out of the decision-making process. All arrangements were handled by him and my Jehovah's Witness siblings.

Now I had to fight to go to the funeral. I wondered how I could manage getting out of going, because why should I pay a bunch of money on travel expenses and lost income to be around and deal with the rest of my shitty, dysfunctional family, telling me how sorry they are for the loss of our mother? I had gone through decades of intense grief and upset when she cut me out of her life, without a shred of support or care from many of them who would be there. I was sick with the thought of facing four out of seven Jehovah's Witness siblings. I wondered how I was going to feel sitting at her funeral, plastering a phony smile on my face in front of the very people who hate me, without feeling like a total hypocrite.

And then the thought of my father came to my mind. To me, it would be even more preposterous for me to offer sympathy to a man whose marriage to my mother had been sixty-two years of hell, and who was instrumental in breaking up our relationship and influencing her to disown me up until the day she died.

Furthermore, at best, my family will try to "bury the hatchet" under false pretenses without ever getting anything resolved, and the reconciliation will be short-lived. So, what's the point of it all? They proved that after my sister died, as mentioned earlier. Everyone went their separate ways and now here we were again. But there was one thing that I did know; my heart would tell me what to do when making a decision such as this; a decision I dreaded having to make.

Once deciding to attend, I drew up a plan. One thing I wasn't going to do was be around the same people who had banished me all my life. I didn't want to be seen by them, so I decided that I would go early, before anyone else, and view her body alone. I would then make my exit. Since the burial was only a few blocks away, I would drive to the gravesite and wait until everyone left to have a moment alone with my mother.

Then suddenly, I had a God moment. I had to follow through with what he had put on my heart. I immediately became aware of my present circumstances and the reality that I needed to change my mind. Light penetrated my darkness, and I realized that there was something that exists that was far more profound than I, and I needed to attend the services for various reasons. Many family members who had hurt me over the years were also hurting themselves, and I needed to open my heart to them regardless of how they really felt about me.

While advocating for what was best for my mother, I thought it would be wise to let go of anger and resentment towards them and strive for the undeniable peace that comes from acceptance and forgiveness; neither stifling my impulse to call out an uncooperative brother or sister, nor allowing myself to be consumed with anger. I was not going with an agenda to make statements to family members or to try to confront past family issues. There was no way I was going to gag myself with that kind of behavior.

In times of grief, old differences are forgotten, and all that matters is that I was once an important person in my mother's life. Now was the time to be supportive and not bring up any bad blood. Being a gentleman of tact, respect, and sensitivity was more important than adding distractions and stress. Regardless of how they felt about me, I'd do things because they're right and good, and because my desire to serve others supersedes my own comfort.

Furthermore, if I didn't go, I would never have a chance for a do-over. At the end of the day, my job was very simple; be a man of honor, be supportive and dignified. So, I decided to go and stay for the whole service and give support to my family, especially my children; I could not leave them at such a critical time.

In Jersey City, New Jersey, in the heart of the ghetto, I saw garbage as its standout feature. Blunt wrappers, McDonald's cartons, Magnum wrappers, soiled Kotex maxi pads, broken glass, and the utmost in ghetto garbage. I drove to my father's place of worship in the black community, located on Martin Luther King Jr. Drive, and it was no different. What I saw was totally unbelievable. I didn't know I had to play hopscotch over trash when going to view my mother's body, especially in front of a so-called place of worship (the Kingdom Hall).

It's hard to ascertain exactly how much filth and dog shit I saw; it was everywhere. Everywhere you walked you had to watch your step. It was obnoxious and gross. It was like attending a funeral at the local garbage dump. It seemed that the residents of that community were apparently unfazed by it. Then again, nothing had changed since I was a kid preaching in the same neighborhoods; I should have expected it.

As the family gathered together, everyone was trying to pretend that we were a normal family, but the truth revealed the dysfunction; especially as we headed to the Kingdom Hall in separate cars. Usually most families gather together in a family car or a limousine. With my family, we were scattered around like mice in a maze. We didn't walk into the place of service as a family. My selfish father even drove his own vehicle and didn't give a rat's ass about the rest of the family.

As I entered the Kingdom Hall, it seemed that all heads turned to me. Once seated, I felt every pair of eyes on me, burning a hole in the back of my skull. Many hadn't seen me in decades. Yet, the treatment I received varied. Some gave me hugs, and several others came up to speak to me. However, the majority refused to approach me, and specifically avoided any eye contact. I guess that "under the circumstances" they were there to give their condolences, nothing else!

Next was my father. I saw him for the coward he was. I saw him as a man who was terrified of feelings. How could I expect my feelings to be validated by this man when he wasn't even willing to validate his own? He just sat there, cold as ice, saying nothing, not even acknowledging my existence. I really felt sorry for him because of his own inability to connect with me in a way that would have been good for him. Much of my adult life had been spent worrying about how I could rescue him, free him from an organization that kept him shackled mentally; and right there, in the Kingdom Hall, he had the opportunity for self-encounter, for a journey we could undertake as father and son—and his courage failed. He pushed the truth away, fleeing back to what is toxic and familiar; I am the problem; I am dis-fellowshipped. I am the crooked nail.

It is a shame that even during such a difficult time, the *Watchtower* society feels determined to impose its irrational behavior on others. I have been out of the religion long enough, and been confronted by shunning often enough, to have been prepared to handle this type of craziness.

My mother's coffin was displayed in the Kingdom Hall, which was filled with Jehovah's Witnesses. After family and friends viewed her body during the wake, we were all asked to stand and together sing a boring Jehovah's Witness song. The song was printed on back of the program and came from the Jehovah's Witness songbook entitled *See Yourself When All is New*. The group sang together a cappella. The song lacked passion, was very dull and unenthusiastic; unenthusiastic because it wasn't a Christian song, one that's anointed with the Holy Spirit of Jesus. Anyone would fall asleep while listening to such rubbish. I wish I could have invited a church choir to sing for my mother; they would have done a much better job. But at the Kingdom Hall, no non-Witness religious songs would have been allowed to be sung or played.

Then the empty talk began. The family sat together and listened to a *Watchtower* minister preach her funeral. It was a rerun of my sister's memorial. He parroted what he had been taught and what he read in the material. As he continued, I was just amazed how confined and limited his thinking was. Much of it sounded like he was talking to a class of elementary school children.

As the funeral progressed, I found myself disappointed and irritated at the proceedings. There was no talk about how good of a mom, sister, wife, grandmother, great-grandmother, and friend to many people she was. The speaker didn't tell us what she was passionate about in life. He said nothing to add to her treasure box of memories. All we heard was Jehovah this and Jehovah that. I was so incensed I could hardly keep from expressing the thoughts that had been boiling in my heart throughout the sermon. I had to resort to silence as a protection against outrage.

The value of my mother was apparently only thirty minutes' worth, twenty-eight of which were spent giving a "fine witness." It was an opportunity for the elder to stage an infomercial about the organization to a captive audience of unconverted suspects who may be attending; utterly tasteless. He did it with total disregard for the sanctity of human life. For the last twenty-eight minutes, he belabored his point about the benefits of joining the Watchtower organization. Jehovah's Witnesses don't understand that a funeral is supposed to be about remembering the deceased. It should not be used as a multi-level marketing event. I mean, damn! Pull that crap at Sunday meetings, not when I'm trying to grieve for my mother!

Lo and behold, the dork of a speaker started in with the impending resurrection abysmal speech, where the dead come back to life as zombies with new bodies and new minds living in a "paradise" setting. Mom was not good enough to go to heaven. She had an earthly hope; nothing more, nothing less. The speaker was totally apathetic. The Jehovah's Witness elder started reading First Thessalonians chapter 4 out of the *Watchtower*'s own New World Translation of the Scripture:

"Moreover, brothers, we do not want you to be ignorant concerning those who are sleeping [in death]; that you may not sorrow just as the rest also do who have no hope. For if our faith is that Jesus died and rose again, so, too, those who have fallen asleep [in death] through Jesus God will bring with him" (1 Thess. 4:13-14, NWT).

But I had a big problem with him not finishing the entire Scripture. Even in their own New World Translation of the Scripture it reads:

131

"For this is what we tell you by Jehovah's word, that we the living who survive to the presence of the Lord shall in no way precede those who have fallen asleep [in death]; because the lord himself will descend from heaven with a commanding call, with an archangel's voice and with God's trumpet, and those who are dead in union with Christ will rise first. Afterward we the living who are surviving will, together with them, be caught away in clouds to meet the lord in the air; and thus, we shall always be with [the] lord. Consequently, keep comforting one another with these words" (1 Thess. 4:15-18, NWT).

If he was a true Christian; you would think that he would quote the whole Scripture. But the Jehovah's Witnesses don't believe that your soul returns to the Creator at death. Therefore, there was no rejoicing for my mother being reunited with lost loved ones, as Christianity proclaims.

He went on to say that Sister Thomas would not know any conscious existence until the resurrection, at which time she would be judged, and Jehovah would determine if she was to have eternal life on earth. But like the fake minister he is, he is not in harmony with what the Bible says.

"To be absent from the body is to be present with the Lord" (2 Cor. 5:8).

The falsehood that causes a soul to be eternally lost is far more deadly than any earthly poison. The stupidity of his sermon was incredible. The whole arrangement was absolutely disgusting. I've never been made physically sick just being in a situation in that way. I still can't wrap my head around how disrespectful the whole thing was. Yet, I had to sit there and endure this bunch of apathy. I squirmed in my seat for the rest of the service.

After the final prayer and all was said and done, family members and friends were not permitted to reminisce about her. Jehovah's Witnesses don't like anyone who is not a Witness speaking from the podium at their Kingdom Halls because they like to have complete control. They sure weren't going to let me up on the podium out of fear that I would use it as a platform to turn people away from their fake faith.

All I wanted to do was pay respect to my mother and have the opportunity to say goodbye the way I wanted to say goodbye. She had been lied to, deceived, and her life was stolen. I didn't see anything wrong with saying a few nice things about her before her body was buried. Maybe some family members would have liked to have played her favorite song. Perhaps even show some videos or photos on a screen that tell the story of her life; Jehovah's Witness, or some other aspect of that. Perhaps some of us would like to have shared with others what her favorite foods were, where she liked to go for vacation, what kind of work she did, etc. Not being allowed to do that from an organization that claims to represent Jesus Christ was a downright dirty shame. So, we all sat there in silence; reduced to the lowest term like a fraction. You can't get more heartless and unsympathetic than that!

Looking over at my father, I willed him to step up to the plate for me, for my mom, for my sister, for my brother, for his grandsons, for himself; but I was kidding myself because the way he acted fitted the tone of the relationship he had with the family, or lack thereof. I took it up with him later and asked why he couldn't be a little more sympathetic to his grieving family. Then again, I already knew the answer; as with my deceased sister, it was not in his custom to honor a deceased family member...period. Shameless!

Furthermore, as I sat there staring into space, the thought came to my mind that I needed to put something in my will so my family wouldn't pull this obnoxious act if something were to happen to me. I don't want my friends and coworkers confused at my funeral. I can never imagine my children and grandchildren not honoring my transition. When I pass, they will have the option to not have it officiated by anyone. I think they would like people to know about their father and grandfather, humorous stories about me and not a lecture about any organization and recruitment to join them. My greatest obligation is to leave a good impression on them; positive beliefs and behavior that they can carry forward.

While at the gravesite, as we surrounded my mother's coffin waiting for the interment, I had hoped my father took my earlier advice to have my sister's ashes buried in the same grave. He had said that it was a good idea. At the end of the day, he gave a cock and bull story that it was against the law because they viewed her ashes as another body and would charge him. Although that might be true, the shameful truth is that to him, she was dis-fellowshipped and would spoil my mother's chances of having an earthly resurrection. To me, that said it all!

Finally, in many faiths, sending flowers to the funeral home or the home of those who have lost a loved one is a kind gesture and an appropriate sympathy gift. However, after many years of faithful service by my mother, no flowers were sent by the *Watchtower* society or the Jehovah's Witness congregation she belonged to. God's so-called chosen people would not even send donations to help honor her memory.

I left the services angry and insulted. My feelings and grief were not acknowledged or addressed; nor was there any closure. I did not attend the social aspects at my dad's house, just the repast. It was painful to see the family get together only after a loved one had died. I also knew how Dad thought, and that mattered to me. I know his religious beliefs, and he would not have wanted me there; I wasn't invited.

Hopefully, he will call a meeting of the Witness side of the family (almost equally divided; all raised Jehovah's Witnesses, some never baptized, some now capable of seeing the failings of the organization) and finally admit to us that he has been terribly misused and lied to, and that it is time to face the truth that the Jehovah's Witness Bible is the faulty word of men (the Governing Body of Jehovah's Witnesses). Hopefully he will tell everyone that it's time to put away hatred and reunite our family. Then again, perhaps I am disillusioned in expecting anything different from him.

I don't see him stepping forward to have any kind of a relationship after my mother's passing. Three year and a half after her death, he continues to proceed from a false assumption; he's afraid of bruising his ego and admitting he made a mistake in joining the cult. The truth be told, when you come from a dysfunctional, narcissistic family, nothing never changes for the best. He will never apologize, never ask for forgiveness, and never attempt to absolve himself. He will go to his grave content in the knowledge that he did his best to destroy me and others while projecting his false image to the world as a perfect Jehovah's Witness slave.

Until that time, he can continue to judge me for the rest of his days if he so wishes, but I will have no more of it. My time/love/energy is valuable, and I am no longer giving it to those who don't value me. Love is not pain. If love hurts, it probably isn't love. Love should add value, not take away.

As far as some of my Jehovah's Witness siblings are concerned, they won't budge, either, because their minds have been set on spin dry and forgotten. They also are to reflect what Dad likes about himself. I don't know that they will ever want to find their way out of those roles. It would take a lot for them to acknowledge that they are Witness slaves and make the drastic changes required to relate to other non-Witness family members who can clearly see their chains.

Freedom requires responsibility, and freedom is worth it to me, to take that responsibility. What they don't realize is that the ones who stand up to the abuse, dysfunction, disorders, and inappropriate behavior are the noble, strong, intelligent, and special people who will break an extremely harmful and damaging trend in the family and cause a ripple of positive change that will last for generations to come. I feel for them, love them, and miss them, but I don't have much hope for them to break free.

I look in the mirror and think of all the ways I can be a better human being. My heart is often filled with great sorrow and loneliness. Yet I have been making a conscientious effort to be kinder, generous, caring, and more empathetic to everyone. As mentioned earlier, one thing my mother taught me was to be kind to others, and I will not let her down! The world will see the light that she had brought into the world. No matter what evil men (the *Watchtower* society) told her about me, her light will shine through me, regardless of what has been said.

After my mother's death, I fulfilled a vow to visit and place flowers on her grave. It took me a while because all that has taken place, circumstances had caused me to lose my joy, but not my love for her. Hurt feelings has robbed me of so much in my life, but before I could make a move to her grave, I had to be ready; I had to take the hurt out, dismiss what she had done. To me, it didn't matter what she had done but how I respond. Showing mercy and forgiveness and passion, brought closure, leaving used abused and forgotten behind. The mind is said to be the human consciousness that originates in the brain and is manifested in thoughts, perception, emotion, will, memory, and imaginations. The heart is the seat of our emotion and the memory of my mother is still locked up in my heart forever.

I have strong spiritual belief that helps me to overcome most sadness and difficult situations. There are many love-filled Christians, as well as other religions, everywhere in this world and I have found a place to fellowship with them. Spending the last half of my life trying to demonstrate to others that there may be something worth investigating in even the most seemingly wonderful belief system is my way of giving back what was taken from me. My family situation makes me more dedicated to serving and giving to those who need guidance, help and support.

I extend my heart to anyone who wishes to contact me. I would gladly assist Jehovah's Witnesses and ex-Witnesses in an effort to deprogram themselves from this destructive, mind-controlling cult.

What I experienced has made an indelible mark on my spirit, and it's good to know that I will not be processing that experience into eternity, but receiving the love and understanding of the Supreme Being. I would rather be dead than in bondage of any kind.

It's nice to know that my accountability isn't to some Jehovah's Witness god that can never be satisfied, but to myself, my children, my friends, and my community. I am very grateful for my life, and I'm looking forward to a future that is sculpted according to what I need and want. The quality and fullness of my life cannot be expressed in words.

While I live my life out of the *Watchtower* society, even though it's without family, I am also trying to keep them in my prayers. But I also know that I must face realty and accept that it seems at this point, the situation will never be resolved. Therefore, I must find and create whatever peace I desire in my own life and my own heart. I love them, but know they will not accept or feel my love, so I must move on to someone else who does.

"Come unto me, all ye that labour and are heavy laden, and I will give you rest. Take my yoke upon you, and learn of me; for I am meek and lowly in heart: and ye shall find rest unto your souls. For my yoke is easy, and my burden is light (Matt. 11:28-30). I am the door of the sheep. All that ever came before me are thieves and robbers: but the sheep did not hear them.... By me if any man enters in, he shall be saved, and shall go in and out, and find pasture. The thief cometh not, but for to steal, and to kill, and to destroy: I am come that they might have live, and that they might have it more abundantly" (John 10:7-10).

In 1981, Lloyd John Ogilvie wrote a book called *God's Best for My Life*. His insightful words help me come to this fitting conclusion of my journey to make further peace with the past:

"We all need power. We need an inner energizing of our minds and wills. We were meant to be recreated to be like Jesus. We cannot do it on our own, but he is able! The indwelling Christ, the power at work in us, infuses the tissues of our brains with a vivid picture of the person we can become. Then He guides each decision and discernment of our wills. He shows us how we are to act and react as new creatures. Our depleted energies are engendered with strength. We actually have supernatural power to think, act, and respond with infused capacities."

So, that's my story. I again thank God for permitting me to share with you the history of my life, to spread the word about this hushed-up subject of the Jehovah's Witnesses, to never, ever let what happened to me and those like me, ever be repeated upon any human. It was incredibly damaging to be taught to second-guess yourself at every turn, to be taught to follow the advice of others instead of your own counsel, and to be henpecked to death with judgments that leave you questioning your worth as a human being.

This book was an introduction to who I was and have become today. Despite being used abused and forgotten, after my journey, I rose and overcame it. I survived and was able to control who I became and the life I wanted to live. As I began focusing on myself for once, trying not to think about the past, I began working out, and I feel great! I'm now redirecting the confidence and beauty I felt from within. I feel alive again and have transformed myself. The transformation includes physical, mental, psychological, and spiritual boundaries involving beliefs, emotions, intuitions, and self-esteem. Knowing what I am and who I am gives me freedom. If I did not own my life, my choices and options would have become limited. The truth was always in front of me and what I needed to tell my story in order to make me stronger, to bring me to where I am now, to know where I needed to grow and what is next for me. I found out who I was because I did not know who I was at first. But in the quest of knowing, I found myself. It was time I became a better me. After being used abused and forgotten, I started these 24 affirmations:

"I am good enough."
"I am handsome."
"I am confident in who I am."
"I release negativity."
'I fill my mind with positive thoughts."
"I attract such beauty into my life."
"I am healthy and happy."
"I love me just the way I am."
'I am comfortable in my own skin."
"I am free of negativity."
'I like the person I am becoming."
"I love all aspects of my body."
"I think positive thoughts about myself and others."
"I validate myself on a daily basis."
"I have an attractive mind, body, and spirit."
"I like the person I see in the mirror."

"My natural beauty shines forth."
'Feeling good about myself is my natural birthright."
"I confront what I need to do with love in my heart."
"I have the inner strength to face life."
"I have all the willpower I need."
"Each day I focus on my inner strength."
"I protect myself against any hurt that comes my way."
"I love who God has made me to be."

Like the soap opera tells us, "Like sands through the hourglass, so are the days of our lives." I found that by broadening my horizons and focusing less on what the Jehovah's Witnesses did to me, I could then discover more things about myself. And while I am happy, I know that my journey is in no way complete. Yet, I live in freedom and I live and love!

I believe that in my lifetime, say the next 10 years, I'll see a collapse of this faux religion. It will crumble, or be just another interesting historic footnote of the Adventist movement started in the 1800s. Until that time, in my flight for justice, before I reach the end of my earthly journey and lay down to my final rest, I will fulfill the most cherished dreams of my later years; exposing them for who they really are: wolves in sheep's' clothing. I shall be devoted to an unceasing warfare against the accursed shame of the organization and those who tried to destroy me as a human being and rob me of having a relationship with my family based on unconditional love.

In the end, I have gained far more than I have lost. All the frustration and unhappiness helped spur my creativity, which now helps me make a living. I'm an author, a retired law enforcement officer, a certified suicide prevention councilor, youth advocate instructor, and a certified personal trainer for older people with chronic conditions. I also have a great sense of humor. I think a great sense of humor was crucial to my recovery from anything negative in my life. It has helped me tremendously in being successful and happy.

## Chapter 15: The Final Act

Thank you for allowing me to ramble on and get some of these thoughts out of my system. Please keep me and my family in your prayers. I have emancipated myself from the Jehovah's Witnesses, spiritually, emotionally, and intellectually, and I have told this story to fulfill my mission on this behalf.

www.ingramcontent.com/pod-product-compliance
Lightning Source LLC
Chambersburg PA
CBHW072349090426
42741CB00012B/2980